NEW DIRECTIONS FOR EVALUATION
A PUBLICATION OF THE AMERICAN EVALUATION ASSOCIATION

Gary T. Henry, *Georgia State University*
COEDITOR-IN-CHIEF

Jennifer C. Greene, *University of Illinois*
COEDITOR-IN-CHIEF

Responsive Evaluation

Jennifer C. Greene
University of Illinois

Tineke A. Abma
Erasmus University

EDITORS

Number 92, Winter 2001

JOSSEY-BASS
San Francisco

RESPONSIVE EVALUATION
Jennifer C. Greene, Tineke A. Abma (eds.)
New Directions for Evaluation, no. 92
Jennifer C. Greene, Gary T. Henry, Coeditors-in-Chief
Copyright ©2001 John Wiley & Sons, Inc.

Microfilm copies of issues and articles are available in 16mm and 35mm, as well as microfiche in 105mm, through University Microfilms Inc., 300 North Zeeb Road, Ann Arbor, Michigan 48106-1346.

New Directions for Evaluation is indexed in Contents Pages in Education, Higher Education Abstracts, and Sociological Abstracts.

Print ISSN: 1097-6736;   Online ISSN: 1534-875X;   ISBN: 0-7879-5794-1

NEW DIRECTIONS FOR EVALUATION is part of The Jossey-Bass Education Series and is published quarterly by Jossey-Bass, 989 Market Street, San Francisco, California 94103-1741.

SUBSCRIPTIONS cost $69.00 for U.S./Canada/Mexico; $93 international. For institutions, agencies, and libraries, $145 U.S.; $185 Canada; $219 international. Prices subject to change.

EDITORIAL CORRESPONDENCE should be addressed to the Editors-in-Chief, Jennifer C. Greene, Department of Educational Psychology, University of Illinois, 260E Education Building, 1310 South Sixth Street, Champaign, IL 61820, or Gary T. Henry, School of Policy Studies, Georgia State University, P.O. Box 4039, Atlanta, GA 30302-4039.

www.josseybass.com

Printed in the United States of America on acid-free recycled paper containing 100 percent recovered waste paper, of which at least 20 percent is postconsumer waste.

NEW DIRECTIONS FOR EVALUATION

Sponsored by the American Evaluation Association

Editorial Policy and Procedures

New Directions for Evaluation, a quarterly sourcebook, is an official publication of the American Evaluation Association. The journal publishes empirical, methodological, and theoretical works on all aspects of evaluation. A reflective approach to evaluation is an essential strand to be woven through every volume. The editors encourage volumes that have one of three foci: (1) craft volumes that present approaches, methods, or techniques that can be applied in evaluation practice, such as the use of templates, case studies, or survey research; (2) professional issue volumes that present issues of import for the field of evaluation, such as utilization of evaluation or locus of evaluation capacity; (3) societal issue volumes that draw out the implications of intellectual, social, or cultural developments for the field of evaluation, such as the women's movement, communitarianism, or multiculturalism. A wide range of substantive domains is appropriate for *New Directions for Evaluation;* however, the domains must be of interest to a large audience within the field of evaluation. We encourage a diversity of perspectives and experiences within each volume, as well as creative bridges between evaluation and other sectors of our collective lives.

The editors do not consider or publish unsolicited single manuscripts. Each issue of the journal is devoted to a single topic, with contributions solicited, organized, reviewed, and edited by a guest editor. Issues may take any of several forms, such as a series of related chapters, a debate, or a long article followed by brief critical commentaries. In all cases, the proposals must follow a specific format, which can be obtained from the editor-in-chief. These proposals are sent to members of the editorial board and to relevant substantive experts for peer review. The process may result in acceptance, a recommendation to revise and resubmit, or rejection. However, the editors are committed to working constructively with potential guest editors to help them develop acceptable proposals.

Jennifer C. Greene, Coeditor-in-Chief
Department of Educational Psychology
University of Illinois
260E Education Building
1310 South Sixth Street
Champaign, IL 61820
e-mail:jcgreene@uiuc.edu

Gary T. Henry, Coeditor-in-Chief
School of Policy Studies
Georgia State University
P.O. Box 4039
Atlanta, GA 30302-4039
e-mail: gthenry@gsu.edu

CONTENTS

EDITORS' NOTES

With the address titled *"Program Evaluation, Particularly Responsive Evaluation,"* given during a sabbatical in Sweden in 1973, Robert Stake offered a new vision and rationale for educational and social program evaluation to the then-fledgling evaluation communities (Stake, [1973] 1987). In this vision, evaluation was reframed—from the application of sophisticated analytic techniques that address distant policymakers' questions of program benefits and effectiveness "on the average," to an engagement with on-site practitioners about the quality and meanings of their practice. These innovative ideas helped accelerate a transformation of the evaluation enterprise into its current pluralistic character, within which remain multiple and varied legacies of key responsive evaluation principles. This volume offers some of these legacies.

The legacies are recounted in the diverse and distinctive voices of the authors. These authors have been selected for this volume because their lives and their work have intersected with the pathways forged by Bob Stake. The authors all make sense of the ideas and tenets of responsive evaluation from their own locations in the evaluation field. These locations and thus these voices include the abstract, idea-laden arguments of theory and philosophy; the personalized reminiscences of past experience; the value-driven, politicized demands of activism; and the dissonant discourses of postmodern skepticism. The very presence of multiple, diverse voices is highly congruent with the pluralism of responsiveness. And so are these authors' successful efforts to write authentically from their own location rather than hide their authorship behind the mask of convention, to create metaphors to convey complex ideas, to use imagery to invoke readers' imagination, and to tell stories that invite readers to vicariously share in the experiences and convictions being recounted. In this volume, then, style is more than an aesthetic curiosity. The distinctive styles of the various chapters represent the authors' desire to be consistent, to write in such a way that the text reflects important underlying values and ideas.

Through these various chapter authors, the aim of this volume is to trace some of the influences of responsive evaluation on the contemporary practice and theory of evaluation and related domains of inquiry. Though many of the authors provide their own critique of key ideas in responsive evaluation and while some offer examples from practice, this volume is not designed to offer a comprehensive critique of responsive evaluation nor to offer guidelines for its application in practice. Instead, the various authors have initiated a dialogue with Stake's work on responsive evaluation, a dialogue we hope will continue in other forums and venues.

An introductory chapter presents responsive evaluation's core ideas, as anchored in the original visions of Robert Stake and the evolution of his thought over a period of thirty-five years. Excerpts from Stake's interviews with Tineke Abma and from his published work punctuate this discussion. In Chapter Two, Ernest House offers some personal reflections on his own early engagement with the liberating ideas and field experiences of responsive evaluation, particularly its orientation to local stakeholder issues, populist and pluralistic value stances, and qualitative methodology. For House, Stake's work offered institutional and intellectual legitimization for these ideas. For House, however, Stake's work was also limited by its value relativity and its ultimate reliance on the judgments of the evaluator-as-arbiter. House's own "deliberative democratic" approach to evaluation rejects such relativism in favor of "dialogue and deliberation procedures as rational tests of [the] validity" of competing stakeholder evaluative claims.

The next two chapters also engage the political dimensions of responsive evaluation. In Chapter Three, Stafford Hood argues that "to be responsive fundamentally means to attend substantively and politically to issues of culture and race in evaluation practice." Hood then provides historical documentation of the significant work of early African American educational evaluators. He argues that this work is neither known nor acknowledged by the mainstream evaluation community, despite (or perhaps because of) its responsiveness to issues of culture and race at that time. This argument clearly demonstrates that responsive evaluation has multiple historical roots. Arguing further that "shared lived experience" is a key facet of effective responsive evaluation, Hood concludes with a powerful summons for more evaluators of color in our community.

Yoland Wadsworth recounts in Chapter Four her own personal story of becoming responsive as an evaluator—a story that also focuses on the inclusion of marginalized voices in evaluation. Wadsworth has practiced evaluation as an activist, change-oriented inquirer in the domains of human services and community development. She found early on the need to include service deliverers and especially end users "compelling and simultaneously bewilderingly difficult." Wadsworth's chapter traces the evolution of her endeavors to develop processes for effective stakeholder inclusion and voice, for meaningful interaction and dialogue, and thereby for the possibility of democratizing action and change. Wadsworth acknowledges her work as a political departure from Stake's original ideas of evaluation audience and evaluator stance, yet as *her* response to the mandate to reknit community by acknowledging difference and finding common commitments.

In Chapter Five, Ian Stronach presents a postmodern reading of Stake's work. He focuses on the work's "self-betrayal" and illuminates several tensions therein. One is the stated intention to be responsive and open to stakeholder issues on one hand, and the advocacy for things personally cherished by the evaluator on the other. Another tension is the intention to be responsive using an emergent design on one hand, and the specific direction offered by methods on the other. Stronach interprets these tensions as symptomatic of the undesirability of *any* model or methodology for the practice of evaluation. But his postmodern rejoinder to responsive evaluation "is not rejection; it is a reanimation and a continuing creation." We acknowledge that the postmodern discourse in this chapter may be challenging for some readers. We encourage all to take on this challenge as Stronach's messages are provocative and important.

Like Stronach, Thomas Schwandt in Chapter Six focuses on the extra-methodological dimensions of responsive evaluation. Schwandt argues for interpreting Stake's work as "an effort to encourage evaluators to capitalize on our everyday ways of making sense of the value of social and educational programs." In lieu of exclusive reliance on technical knowing and proce-dural rationality, Schwandt interprets responsiveness as also embracing tacit and experiential knowing, "attention to the texture and concrete details of people's experiences," as well as "moral and political speculation, critique, interpretation, dialogue, and judgment." Responsive evaluation thus defines a middle ground "between overreliance on and overapplication of method, general principles, and rules to making sense of ordinary life, on one hand, and advocating trust in personal inspiration and sheer intuition, on the other."

In the final chapter, Linda Mabry demonstrates the applicability of responsive evaluation's core ideas to other domains, in this case, person-alized assessment in the field of education. Just as responsive evaluation attends to local stakeholder interests and contextual perceptions and expe-riences, personalized assessment responds to each student's individual interests and unique accomplishments. Mabry organizes her argument through creative multiple-choice analogies, for example, "personalized assessment is to responsive evaluation as . . . (b) Harpo is to Groucho." Mabry acknowledges that contextualized, detailed portrayals of program quality and of student achievement "are minor players" on today's stage of normative, expert-driven demands for accountability (because, for example, they fail to facilitate comparison to external referents). Their value, she argues, is in "their respect for students, teachers, and stake-holders as the proper locus of judgment and control regarding their own lives and professional endeavors."

The work of Egon Guba and Yvonna Lincoln also has intellectual and political roots in Stake's explicit work on responsive evaluation. For Guba and Lincoln his work meant not only a significant change in evaluation focus, but also a fundamental paradigm shift from positivism to construc-tivism (Abma, 1994). Hostility and indifference in the field stimulated them to develop a "methodological sub-tract" that was intended to make Stake's approach acceptable in the conventional academic domain. Guba and Lin-coln also developed their own "responsive-constructivist" or "negotiation" approach to evaluation. From Lincoln's perspective it was not until 1989, when *Fourth Generation Evaluation* was published, that Stake's initial ideas and arguments—expressed in an ordinary, nontheoretical, practice-oriented language—were fully explicated conceptually and supported by a cohesive methodology (Abma, 1994). Influenced by feminist and other critical theories and by the recognition that situations are often characterized by unequal power constellations, Lincoln (1993) later explicitly promoted an "open-ideological position" in which the evaluator should pay deliberate attention to and become an advocate of silenced voices.

As narrated in this volume, the legacies of responsive evaluation include both artistic and political dimensions. The *artistic* dimension emphasizes the aesthetic, relational, and moral facets of our craft, and thus the contextual, contingent, unfinished aspects of our evaluative claims. For Ian Stronach "art triumphs" over method because, in Stake's words, evaluation is "an advocacy for those things we cherish." For Thomas Schwandt, evaluation is practical wisdom, requiring not the application of technical procedures but rather attentiveness to the particulars of the situation, to the lived reality of practice. And Linda Mabry advances personalized assessment precisely because it values the concrete experiences and unique attainments of individual students. These authors read Stake's work as a rejection of methodological directives in favor of attending to lived experience, the unexpected, the individual, and the beautiful.

Reflecting the *political* dimension of responsive evaluation, Ernest House, Stafford Hood, and Yoland Wadsworth are all attracted to the democratic potential of Stake's work and read it as enabling a more pluralistic or inclusive approach to evaluation. They extend and transform Stake's work into evaluation approaches that involve not only doing evaluation *for* as many stakeholders as possible, but doing it *with* them through democratic and dialogic processes. While Stake sees and practices the role of evaluator as teacher, they promote and practice the role of evaluator as facilitator and mediator. House, Hood, and Wadsworth each attend specifically to marginalized and politically powerless stakeholder groups, with a vision of using evaluation to redress past wrongs and to further social justice.

In its conceptualization and enactment—as testified by the stature of the contributing authors—this volume is offered in honor of Bob Stake, one of the "uncles of evaluation" (Lincoln, personal communication with Abma, summer 1994). The book he always wanted to write about responsive evaluation has not (yet) appeared. This volume, we hope, begins to fills that space.

Jennifer C. Greene
Tineke A. Abma
Editors

References

Abma, T. A. "Responsive Evaluation, In Conversation with Its Co-creators." Unpublished manuscript, Summer 1994.
Guba, E. G., and Lincoln, Y. S. *Fourth Generation Evaluation*. Thousand Oaks, Calif.: Sage, 1989.

Lincoln, Y. S. "Tracks Towards a Postmodern Politics of Evaluation." Draft of a paper prepared for delivery at the fifth annual conference of the Southeast Evaluation Association, Tallahassee, Fla., Jan. 1993.

Stake, R. E. "Program Evaluation, Particularly Responsive Evaluation." Keynote address at the conference "New Trends in Evaluation," Institute of Education, University of Göteborg, Sweden, Oct. 1973. In G. F. Madaus, M. S. Scriven, and D. L. Stufflebeam (eds.), *Evaluation Models: Viewpoints on Educational and Human Services Evaluation.* Boston: Kluwer-Nijhoff, 1987.

JENNIFER C. GREENE is professor of educational psychology at the University of Illinois, Urbana-Champaign. Her work concentrates on qualitative, participatory, and mixed-method approaches to evaluation.

TINEKE A. ABMA is working at the Department of Health Care Policy and Management of the Erasmus University, Rotterdam, The Netherlands.

1

Responsive evaluation, as a doctrine extending and disciplining common sense, has an intellectual history, some of it passing through Robert Stake's work in the late sixties. That is where this article begins. It is meant to set the context for this special issue, Responsive Evaluation, *by presenting Stake's work. The text is a mosaic of fragments from extensive conversations with Bob Stake in the summer of 1994 and quotes from his older and more recent work. The chapter thus offers a story about Stake's original ideas and their evolution over a period of thirty-five years.*

Stake's Responsive Evaluation: Core Ideas and Evolution

Tineke A. Abma, Robert E. Stake

Sometime in the mid-sixties, common interest and affinity drew together perhaps twenty evaluation scholars in a campus conference room. Recognizing themselves by the date they first met, they called themselves the May 12 Group. They were meeting in the Midwestern United States—more precisely in the Wabash watershed, a beautiful broad valley created by the Wabash River, once a runway for the melting of the great ice flow, dividing and bonding the states of Illinois and Indiana. The May 12 Group faced problems in applying the Tyler (1950) call for goal-oriented evaluation and its mandate to measure the degree to which intended goals had been realized. The conversations went on for many years, with graduate students and faculty of a different university hosting each session. It was Bob Stake who, partly on the basis of a two-day meeting with Michael Scriven, Lee Cronbach, Tom Hastings, and Bob Glaser at CIRCE in 1964, composed a paper—the countenance paper—that reflected the collective state of mind in the field.[1] Not intended as methodology but more as a data inventory, this statement on evaluation featured a comprehensive matrix: six cells for judgment data, six cells for description, and one for the rationale of the program

---

We have chosen to practice a style that reflects Stake's work. What follows is a "thick description" that enables readers to "vicariously experience" what Tineke Abma learned about responsive evaluation in her conversations with Bob Stake. Along the way readers will explore particular concepts and underlying epistemological and political assumptions. The key idea is that if readers have to interpret texts and ideas themselves (in this case, Stake's work), instead of being told how to understand them, they will be more willing to accept and use these ideas in their own contexts.

NEW DIRECTIONS FOR EVALUATION, no. 92, Winter 2001   © John Wiley & Sons, Inc.

(Stake, 1967). Stake (1991) saw it as a plea for broadening the array of data—from only outcomes to antecedents and processes as well.

I was interested in the reasons why Stake was pleading for a wider scope for evaluation at that time, how his argument was received in the field, and how he came up with the idea of responsive evaluation itself—a notion that certainly includes more than just a broadening of the evaluator's scope. In our conversation, Stake took me back to those days:

BOB: The dominant idea then was to look, as Ralph Tyler emphasized, at intended and observed outcomes, just that single comparison. In his own work and writing, one could see a need for doing research on process and background and even judgments. But the way his advice came out, it emphasized data-gathering of two kinds, the goals and the outcomes. A few others, such as Lee Cronbach, were emphasizing that you don't need to compare groups, but mainly find a correlation between inputs and outputs, paying attention to goals and judgments. When I presented the countenance article I wasn't arguing that evaluators should include, in the design, data of all thirteen kinds. From such an array of choices, one should consider carefully what data were needed and perhaps branch out more broadly than before. It still might be that most of the data would fit in just two cells of that matrix, but the idea of legitimizing opportunities to get relevant data of different kinds seemed to me the worth of that paper. I wanted to stretch people's minds as to what should be considered as legitimate data to collect.

TINEKE: How did you move from a widening of the scope of evaluation to responsive evaluation?

BOB: At that time I thought that you didn't need to change your methods of research; you just had to look at additional data that are needed. So you could continue with the quasi-experimental approach or use correlational surveys but be sure to incorporate these additional data. And gradually I realized that we had more different things to do, we had to deal with different issues, deal with different political questions and new questions of validity and legitimacy. By the time I went to Sweden for a sabbatical in 1973 I had a lot of these things in mind and came up with the idea of doing responsive evaluation as more of a methodological guide, not so much an epistemological mapping.

Value Pluralism and Facilitating Judgment Among Local Stakeholders

Early on, Stake pointed out that responsive evaluation assumes value pluralism and that the evaluator should not press for consensus. He put it as follows: "A work of art has no single true value. A program has no single true value. Yet both have value. The value of an art-in-education program will be different for different people, for different purposes. . . . Whatever consensus in values there is . . . should be discovered. The evaluator should not create a consensus that does not exist" (1975a, pp. 25–26).

During our conversations Stake emphasized again that there are different constituencies, different stakeholders who have different expectations, different values. The evaluator should understand those things and be in a good position to illustrate them, to represent them to readers and outsiders as part of the evaluation task. I wanted to know whether or not a responsive evaluation in Stake's opinion should actively include stakeholders in the process of doing evaluation. Who is ultimately making the value judgments?

BOB: The degree to which actors, participants, and subjects being studied should participate in the study is an interesting and difficult question. I see myself frequently now adopting a point of view that I really didn't have before. It came to me from one of the people I studied. I frequently try my designs and interpretations out on them, and I revise. So in fact I am incorporating them into the evaluator role.

TINEKE: OK, but a participatory evaluation would work more deliberately to include and engage people.

BOB: Right, I make strong distinctions between self-study and external responsive evaluation. Self-evaluation may certainly use outsiders, but the locus of control is largely inside. With me, the locus of control needs to stay outside, no matter how much I rely on them. I do not advocate collaborative definition of research questions. To be responsive does not automatically yield design authority to stakeholders. It means coming to know the circumstances and problems and values well, then using professional talent and discipline to carry out the inquiry. For me, the inquiry belongs to the evaluator. She or he conducts it so, in the end, the stakeholders have a good vicarious experience and reconstruction of quality. I do not see the inquiry as a cooperative effort.

TINEKE: [Recalling that responsive evaluation is oriented around the important issues that emerge in the evaluation context] What does this mean for the generation of issues?

BOB: The rhetoric and the ethic of responsive evaluation is to be open, to come to understand what's going on there, to find more than your initial issues. Yet I am struck with how frequently the issues in the final report are matching the original issues. It seems that there is more rigidity in my work than the responsive flexibility I am preaching. For example, I am always concerned about diversity, the particular, and the local, the practitioners and others most close to the program, the problems of standardization.

TINEKE: In the countenance paper you make a distinction between description and judgment. In your later work you no longer portray the judgmental process as an explicit comparison between facts and standards. Could you reflect on the way you conceive the judgmental process?

BOB: In 1964 my thinking was quite analytic and I thought that you should be as explicit as you possibly could be. Gradually I made the change, I don't know how. Now I think of the judgmental act as part of the descriptive, part of the observational act. You see something and simultaneously you have a notion of what it is and how good it is. We might think a little more descriptively at one moment and more judgmentally at another moment, maybe those things go back and forth in our mind, but descriptors and values come out largely at the same time. When you review them the next day or a year later, you may invent some new interpretations. But judgment was present from the first. Also I wanted to include in evaluation theory the idea that the most important judge will often be someone other than the evaluator. The reader, the client, the people outside need to be in a position to make their own judgments, using grounds they have already, plus the new data. I was anxious to set up a strong responsibility for description, to provide the reader with relatively raw data, with fresh opportunities to think about the quality of this evaluand. I never gave up the evaluator's responsibility to provide summary judgments, but I provide them softly framed so as to encourage the reader's own interpretations. *[See also Stake, 1997a.]*

TINEKE: Why is it so important for you to leave the decision making with the audience?

BOB: Because I don't have confidence in analytic procedures' separating setting standards and making observations and action. I think decision making is part of the same act and if a judgment is going to be used by the client or the reader, that person should be engaged in that holistic procedure, to combine observations and interpretations and judgments all in one. You see, I am a populist, a localist. I am fearful of central authority and of connoisseur-control. I see formal evaluation as centralizing, as conservative and working more for the powers that exist than for the powers that should exist. Both reformers and protectionists can profit from an evaluation study, especially if it aims at informing the public.

TINEKE: So it is a political argument to leave the decision making to the public?

BOB: It's political. But it's epistemological too. Grand theory contributes little to governing education. You need to have local theory. You need to be in touch with the situation in order to make the best judgments. I am a situationalist, thinking that goodness in government, goodness in living, goodness in schooling is strongly dependent on the situation. The fact that many things are similar from community to community, from country to country, doesn't persuade me that epistemologically you want to start with the general. Situations may not be all that unique, but you still want to start with the particular.

Case Studies, Local Knowledge, and Petite Generalizations

In 1978 Stake expressed his preference for case study methods. He argued that knowledge from case studies is concrete and contextual, and open for different interpretations. Case studies are therefore fitted to the natural ways in which people assimilate information and come to an understanding:

> Case studies are the preferred method of research because they may be epistemologically in harmony with the reader's experience and thus to that person a natural basis for generalization [p. 5]. . . .
> [M]ost case studies feature: descriptions that are complex, holistic, and involving a myriad of not highly isolated variables; data that are likely to be gathered at least partly by personalistic observation; and a writing style that is informal, perhaps narrative, possibly with verbatim quotation, illustration, and even allusion and metaphor. Comparisons are implicit rather than explicit. Themes and hypotheses may be important, but they remain subordinate to the understanding of the case [p. 7].

Later Stake further specified what types of case studies he had in mind, the so-called *intrinsic* versus *instrumental* case studies (Stake, 1994). The primary purpose of an intrinsic case study is to understand a particular *case* rather than to investigate a certain issue (Stake and Mabry, 1995). Context—cultural, organizational, curricular, legal, professional, policy, and collegial—as well as details are said to be important to gain a deep understanding of a particular case. During our conversation we talked about evaluation studies as case studies, different kinds of case studies and the arguments to conduct an intrinsic case study.

Bob: I think it was Cronbach's observation [*referring to Cronbach and others, 1980*] that all evaluation studies are case studies. Still, we do have something called "evaluation research" where more general phenomena or policies are evaluated. Those studies aren't case studies. The program evaluation work I do regularly has a case definition to it. We evaluate some national program or we evaluate change in one particular school.

Tineke: One of the problems people have with case studies is that they are not suitable to make generalizations and to develop theories. You developed the idea of "naturalistic generalization." Can you explain this concept and how you developed that idea?

BOB: Cronbach was important in that regard too. His one sentence— "Generalizations decay"—is one of the great observations in our evaluation literature. In the early days, we were all working for grand generalizations. The way education benefited from research was by applying the general to the local situation. The idea of setting up applied research directly to deal with petite generalizations, the small understandings of local community or situation, seemed then a waste of the energies of researchers.

TINEKE: Because one wouldn't come up with theory?

BOB: Yes. Localist evaluation designs contribute little to formal theory building. You generate a different kind of information: vicarious experience information, narratives, simple descriptions, sharing of impressions more than propositional information.

TINEKE: Is that also part of the popularization of knowledge?

BOB: I think so. It is important for us to include the interpretations of experts, but I want there to be a respect for feelings, emotions, and preferences, some that don't seem logical, lacking justification.

TINEKE: Why are you so much against grand theory?

BOB: Well, I see it as a force that prevents researchers and others from seeing the uniqueness of a local situation. It tends to give too much attention to isolated variables. And the more we have these powerful theories, the less we are interested in the counterexamples. Ultimately a local situation may be described using grand constructs like intelligence, cooperativeness, and the like, but theory pushes us too fast. We have theory because we can't reanalyze every complexity. We have to have simplifications but we can also rely too heavily on them. It's the overuse, the overreliance that troubles me. So I come out on the other side of theory, petite or local theory.

Improvement of Practice Through Vicarious Experience

Stake has always wanted to make a contribution to educational practices such as discovery learning by giving a maximum amount of vicarious experience. The responsive evaluator should present not only the findings but also personal experiences. Vicarious experiences can function as a substitute for those who are missing direct experiences. This does not imply a rejection of formal scientific knowledge, but Stake points out that we often rely too exclusively on that kind of knowledge. We often forget that a disciplined collection of experiences and experiential logic fit natural forms of knowing. The development of practice by a rational application of formal knowledge or by better understanding of oneself is rooted in changes at a more basic level; someone adds new experiences to the existing ones, and these trigger the redefinition of problems and possible solutions. Intuitively someone will start to think about alternative solutions (Stake, 1986). In a paper with Trumbull he describes this in the following way: "We maintain that practice is guided far more by personal knowings, based on and gleaned from personal experience. And change in practice, or resistance to change, is often directly related. Because of this personal aspect it will sometimes be more useful for research to be designed so that research can evoke vicarious experience which leads to improved practice" (Stake and Trumbull, 1982, p. 5). Vicarious experiences will lead to evolutionary changes instead of substitution, and they will support the self-correcting competence of local practices.

Stories and portrayals of people, places, and events are the most appropriate narrative form to create a vicarious experience, because their lifelikeness and concreteness is close to direct, personal experience. To gain an impression of what these portrayals look like, I found it most helpful to look carefully at the case reports published under Stake's leadership (Stake, Bresler, and Mabry, 1991; Stake and others, 1993, 1996, 1997). The following description may also give the reader a clue what Stake has in mind when he talks about portrayals: "We need a reporting procedure for facilitating vicarious experience. We need to portray complexity. We need to convey holistic impression, the mood, and even the mystery of the experience. The program staff or people in the community may be uncertain, and the audiences should feel that uncertainty. Among the better evangelists, anthropologists, and dramatists are those who have developed the art of storytelling. More ambiguity rather than less may be needed in our reports" (Stake, 1975a, p. 23).

I am particularly interested in the educative potential of evaluation and the role of the evaluator in that regard. Stake had the following to say about evaluation and education:

BOB: Cronbach [again referring to Cronbach and others, 1980] was careful to outline the responsibility of evaluators as a teaching responsibility. Within our choices of teaching style we frequently identify two approaches: didactic and discovery learning. We use the term *didactic* to mean delivery of knowledge. In contrast, we use the term *discovery learning* where the responsibility of the teacher is to anticipate things a child can learn under favorable conditions of self-direction. The main responsibility is to arrange a situation where those knowledges, those understandings, are likely to occur. Then the child is more the determiner of learning. Those are two styles that evaluators also have. They can didactically tell their readers what the value of the evaluand is, or they can lay descriptions out in a way that the reader experiences something of the utility and implication of the evaluand—and arrives at his or her own notions of goodness. We evaluators too want to engage in both kinds of teaching, in both kinds of recording, not denying the readers our view of goodness, but allowing plenty of latitude for them to add their own insights to the ones they already have. It may be that the essential understanding already exists, perhaps crudely shaped, in the mind of the reader, and that this new insight, this new set of findings, gives him or her a basis for modifying, and hopefully improving it, reaching a more perfect understanding.

TINEKE: Do you think that that way of knowledge construction is better?

BOB: Often it is better. I spoke about both my political and epistemological commitment to localism. I pointed out that the circumstances of the situation often are determining, determining the goodness and the value and propriety of how education is conducted. I also emphasized organizing evaluation so that it provides opportunity for people in different situations to use the same findings, to apply them to different existing understandings and experience so as to become a personal or local part of the resolution of value. Certainly there are some circumstances where a local community is going to make a hard and fast, difficult, and expensive choice, such as what kind of school building to build or which teacher to hire. Those are hard choices. To help in a situation like that, following a Scriven approach usually is better, but the situations I get into are very different. They are characterized by a wish to come to understand the quality of a given program already operating.

TINEKE: How would you define the role of the evaluator in responsive evaluation?

BOB: Well, I did mention judge, discovery learning teacher, and facilitator.

TINEKE: Change agent?

BOB: No. Change agent is objectionable in implying that evaluation is a success only as change occurs. I don't like that at all. I like the idea that we study a situation partly to decide what to protect, what to cherish. That's not change as most people see it. They are expecting to move up to a higher level of quality, to get rid of some things, to get more. Those changes should not be emphasized more by the evaluator than maintaining the status quo. What surely should be an aim in much educational administration is to slow the deterioration. Many things are getting worse in education, so one of the responsibilities of the evaluator is to help to protect the status quo, to arrest the deterioration. That could be defined as change—to arrest something is a change—but that is not in the minds of most people when they talk about change agents.

Advocacy in Responsive Evaluation

From the beginning Stake has portrayed the responsive evaluator as someone who acts not primarily as an expert, but as a facilitator. He put it as follows: "I admire most the modest evaluator, playing a supportive role, restraining his impulses to advocate, unlike the crusading evaluator, however honestly and forthrightly he announces his commitments. . . . I emphasize the facilitator-role more than deliverer of insights" (1975b, pp. 36–37).

This is in line with improvement of practice by relying on the specific expertise of practitioners in the local setting. The underlying idea is that those who carry out the program, who are participating in it, have much more knowledge than the evaluator who still has to discover what is going on. Since it is in many fields now accepted that social researchers are implicitly or explicitly promoting certain values in their work, whether it be distance and consensus or engagement, I was interested whether or not Stake has changed his opinion about the role of the evaluator. Is he still skeptical about the evaluator as an advocate of a particular stakeholder group and are there situations where it is unethical not to act as an advocate even if it is in principle unacceptable? We had a heated discussion about this controversial topic:

BOB: The message in the *Handbook [referring to the* Handbook of Qualitative Research *edited by Denzin and Lincoln, 1994]* is that evaluation and qualitative research have a commitment to improvement, to justice, and whatever number of commitments. I am uncomfortable with this message, the coupling of advocacy to evaluation (Stake, 1997b). I know you can't uncouple them entirely, but to urge integration isn't good. Advocative evaluation can't be avoided but should be resisted. We should try to diminish our advocacy rather than to pick out groups that we are most needing to serve. I am, in each study, describing multiple advocacies. I must weigh the merit of each carefully. A friend said that's a recipe for failure; seldom can you be a good advocate of one cause, let alone several. He said each needs to have its own agencies, evaluators, studies that directly, deliberately, carefully, drive home their conceptions and views. I was not persuaded by his argument to omit analysis of multiple advocacies.

TINEKE: In your own work you have always felt more close to practitioners, teachers, nearby stakeholders. Haven't you taken a stance?

BOB: Yes, there is advocacy there. Over my career I have worked more with "nearby" stakeholders, such as parents, and local sponsors rather than distanced ones, not ones who would expect an aggregation over lots of sites in order to make the findings meaningful. I've done some national studies but my frame of reference is the local view, the local perception of quality. So advocacy is there. I don't want to deny that. But, you know, I don't find it useful in the foreword or early paragraphs, to be explicit about my assumptions or standards of goodness, or my advocacies. I don't have a confidence in that mechanism. I think that there are better ways of alerting the reader to biases. . . . Such as putting our own data and interpretation to repeated challenge, to describe the "crucible," and then to remind the reader of our humanity, of our fallibility.

TINEKE: I agree that it is certainly not enough to mention your commitments only in the preface or appendix if you hide behind a mask in the rest of the text. I also recognize what you are saying about the changing commitments with various parties. This is not very comforting and it requires a continuing alertness on the side of the inquirer. How do you decide your position in practice?

BOB: That's a tough question. I face it again and again. For example in Chicago *[referring to Stake, 1997b]* one time I felt that the society at large and the citizens locally should know more about a particular agency, all about its expertise and its flaws. On the other hand, I thought that they would be greatly disserved if I contributed to its termination. I am aware, in political life, that criticism is used in a devastating way. People are forced to give up quickly on things that are of value to them when someone charges them with being objectionable in any way. I have great trouble making the ethical choice.

TINEKE: This is a different tension—between a site and the larger society—from the tension within a site.

BOB: That's true. I think that regularly I escape some of the difficulty by just describing things in sufficient detail so that it is difficult to resolve who is right or who is the party most needing support. I may be overly optimistic that through that kind of impasse, that ambiguity, that people will be prevented from simplistic action.

Constructivist Knowing and Goodness Criteria for Knowledge

In an informal conversation during the summer of 1994 Stake explained that he was lately using the work of René Magritte (see also Stake and Kerr, 1994) to help people to understand the construction of knowledge. Magritte is usually seen as a representative of Surrealism. Stake thinks of him as more than Surrealist, in his own words:

BOB: To me he's a herald of constructivism. I use slices of Magritte's work to illustrate what researchers are doing when they conduct research. Researchers are interpreters of the world. René Magritte was very good at making you think about the process of interpretation and construction. He had the capacity to express doubt. Not the self-doubt that leaves its mark in the paint, but a profound uncertainty about the nature of existence. Flesh turns to wood, marble turns to flesh, skies are ripped, carved up into symmetrical blocks, rocks take the place of clouds, a flash of lightning turns to stone.

Stake talks about inquirers as "provocateurs of understanding" portraying the common in problematic ways. As a provider of images the provocateur reminds us that our words and images are not the experience or object they represent—they are as humanoids from another world. He confronts us with images already formed in the complexity of our innate, tacit experience, to draw attention to our expectations, to shock us out of our day-to-day complacency. Confirmation is not the aim of constructivist research. Instead, like Magritte, it seeks unrealized problems among familiar settings. The interpretation, awareness of the multiplicity of realities is sharpened. Stake conceives the task of an inquirer as follows:

BOB: Like an artist the inquirer is imagining images whose poetry restores to what is known that which is absolutely unknown and unknowable. These provocative images must be presented in "user-friendly" reports, even while being interpretive and provocative. The inquirer must be sensitive to the knowledge and persuasions held by audiences, recognizing appetites for argument, history, dialectic, and extrapolation.

The evaluator does not always act as a provocateur, Stake explains. There are situations in which people already are worried, where there is uncertainty, a lot of variety. Then Stake will not add to that variety but look for unity, for strengths, for good things. This happened to him in Chicago.

I've found it easy to follow Stake's exposé on constructivism, but his writings on relativism and naturalism seemed confusing. Relativism, Stake (1991) wrote, goes before, is prior to naturalism. In response to my question about what he meant, we talked about naturalism, different conceptions of reality, contextualism, goodness criteria for knowledge and procedures.[2]

BOB: When we need inspiration in our evaluation work, we could find it in considering each case, each person, each educational evaluand in its particularity, in its situation. That's the point I am making when I say I am a relativist. Meaning depends on where you are, whom you are working with, what the circumstances are. That is relativism in my lexicon. It's an ideal, a rallying cry. It is more important than attending to national circumstances. National issues are important also but not as important as particularity or relativism.

TINEKE: Relativism means for you that knowledge is context-bound?

BOB: Yes. Relativism means situationalism to me, it is a terribly important aspect of the evaluation work we do.

TINEKE: I understand relativism as opposed to realism, that you are not discovering reality but constructing knowledge in a social context, that's why it is relative. There is no factual reality that can serve as a legitimate ground to validate different experiences and interpretations. We have to accept the multiple character of reality.

BOB: That's good. Yes, that's good.

TINEKE: Somewhere you talk about three types of realities: Reality #1 which we can never know, Reality #2 referring to the commonsense experience of reality, and Reality #3 as the more sophisticated sense of reality. Why do you make a distinction between Reality #2 and #3?

BOB: I want a distinction between description and interpretation, although these two shade into each other. Reality #2 is primarily that reality that we can describe in common with other folks, and see it with a great deal of reliability. It can include intuitive and reflexive recognition, but doesn't go far into implication, into the personal meaning of things. Such elaborations are really Reality #3. I want to keep them separate, because I want to give special attention to the interpretive responsibility that extends beyond description. We need to deal with that descriptive reality without jumping immediately to Reality #3 where interpretations are emphasized.

TINEKE: In a more semiotic or hermeneutic interpretation there are only interpretations.

BOB: Indeed. Well, I could say the uncontested interpretation versus the more controversial interpretation. I wanted to emphasize that there is a reality in which we all participate. This commonly shared reality also is an interpretation. We find little to challenge in that shared reality, much more in our personally interpreted reality.

TINEKE: I found your comments on the relationship between ontology and contextualism also very interesting. You said there is no necessary and determinate relation between relativism and contextualism. There are realists who are also contextualists, for example Yin and Cronbach.

BOB: I think of Yin and Cronbach as weak contextualists. Both are instrumentalists. They believe that you need to take some context into account, because it serves the explanatory value of the study, but getting at the full complexity of the situation is not important to them. The costs of dealing with full description are great, and the payoff is small. Many contextual matters are not measurably related to the action that needs to be taken, not related to the understanding that you are working toward. So they shield their reports from all that noise, from all that sometimes fascinating detail. But the reader often recognizes in that detail some clues to understanding, a little better leverage as to how they want to deal with the issues.

TINEKE: I want to talk about goodness criteria, about validity, reliability, and objectivity. How important is it that we have criteria of goodness?

BOB: We have a strong belief that the criteria of goodness will be shared, will be universal. That's a persuasion we have. But is it a trustworthy persuasion? My answer is, "No, criteria will be diverse." We should keep our criteria of goodness open to change, open to recognition that there are forms of knowledge that we will come to accept only in the future. In time we will be wiser and more willing to change the criteria. In a sense, criteria are evolutionary, they are situational and time-bound, social-system bound. Do you know Umberto Eco's *The Name of the Rose?* *[1983]* In that Italian story, monks from England were successful in undercutting faith in scriptural revelation, substituting observation and logic. Looking back, we now see those times as perverse, with an inferior set of criteria. Now we have a much more durable set but they too are changing. It seems to me, even within my lifetime, paradigms have been changing.

Acceptance of Responsive and Naturalistic Evaluation

Stake has conducted many naturalistic case studies and responsive evaluations. With several other authors I have discussed the opportunities and barriers one may face doing this kind of work in a technocratic society where performance and accountability are becoming more and more dominant (Abma, 1997; Guba and Lincoln, 1981, 1989; Schwandt, 1989). We have pointed out that the profession may fear a loss of authority because an evaluator as knowledge facilitator substitutes for the traditional expert role of the evaluator. Will program managers and policymakers lose their role as neutral decision makers and have to share decision-making power with practitioners and local stakeholders? Will their goals and intentions no longer be the sole criterion and standard to determine value and quality of a program or practice? Detailed portrayals and stories are often considered subjective and particularistic and hence not a sound basis for decision making. On the other hand, people may recognize the worth of gaining an in-depth understanding of the various experiences, multiple realities and evaluations of a case.

I expressed interest in how Stake's work has been accepted and how he deals with eventual resistance within the community of professionals or policymakers. He responded with mixed feelings, finding reason for optimism, but also for pessimism and even cynicism.

BOB: I find much more resistance to responsive evaluation among fellow evaluators than from policymakers, ordinary people, and the public. Ordinary people have an attachment to the idea of a universal Truth, but they are also quick to recognize the inability of researchers or anybody else to get there. They have an expectation of constructed truth. Approximations make them comfortable with the storytelling, with allusion and metaphors.

TINEKE: I've sensed resistance, too.

BOB: Ordinary practitioners, particularly those evaluators able to remain relatively unknown, often have difficulty selling a qualitative design. Some of my students are in trouble when they go out the first couple of times. They need to gain trust and show a portfolio of nice products. Even then the chances are not high.

TINEKE: One last question. You mention in one of your articles how evaluation results are used to legitimate or support certain positions. That is a very cynical observation. Why should we keep on doing evaluations?

BOB: To help keep the spirit of inquiry and reflection alive.

Notes

1. CIRCE is the Center for Instructional Research and Curriculum Evaluation at the University of Illinois, Urbana-Champaign.
2. Philosophical concepts acquire different interpretations both within and across the various theoretical perspectives, and there is no consensus about the meaning of terms such as *relativism* and *naturalism*. The aim here is to disentangle how Stake uses and interprets these concepts. Broadly conceived, *realism* is the doctrine that there are real objects that exist independently of our knowledge of them (Schwandt, 2001, pp. 219–222). *Relativism* refers to the doctrine that denies that there are universal truths. There are several interrelated senses of the terms, however. Schwandt, for example, makes a distinction between epistemological and ontological relativism (2001, pp. 225–226).

References

Abma, T. A. "Playing with/in Plurality, Revitalizing Realities and Relationships in Rotterdam." *Evaluation*, 1997, 5(1), 25–48.

Cronbach, L. J., and others. *Toward Reform of Program Evaluation.* San Francisco: Jossey-Bass, 1980.

Denzin, N. K., and Lincoln, Y. S. (eds.). *Handbook of Qualitative Research.* Thousand Oaks, Calif.: Sage, 1994.

Eco, U. *The Name of the Rose.* New York: Hartcourt Brace, 1983.

Guba, E. G., and Lincoln, Y. S. *Effective Evaluation: Improving the Usefulness of Evaluation Results Through Responsive and Naturalistic Approaches.* San Francisco: Jossey-Bass, 1981.

Guba, E. G., and Lincoln, Y. S. *Fourth Generation Evaluation.* Thousand Oaks, Calif.: Sage, 1989.

Schwandt, T. A. "Recapturing Moral Discourse in Evaluation." *Educational Researcher*, 1989, 18, 11–16.

Schwandt, T. A. *Dictionary of Qualitative Inquiry.* (2nd ed.) Thousand Oaks, Calif.: Sage, 2001.

Stake, R. E. "The Countenance of Educational Evaluation." *Teachers College Record*, 1967, 68(7), 523–540.

Stake, R. E. "To Evaluate an Arts Program." In R. E. Stake (ed.), *Evaluating the Arts in Education: A Responsive Approach.* Columbus, Ohio: Merrill, 1975a.

Stake, R. E. "An Interview with Robert Stake on Responsive Evaluation." In R. E. Stake (ed.), *Evaluating the Arts in Education: A Responsive Approach.* Colombus, Ohio: Merrill, 1975b.

Stake, R. E. "The Case Study Method in Social Inquiry." *Educational Researcher,* 1978, 7, 5–8.

Stake, R. E. "An Evolutionary View of Educational Improvement." In E. R. House (ed.), *New Directions in Education and Evaluation.* London: Falmer, 1986.

Stake, R. E. "Retrospective on `The Countenance of Educational Evaluation.'" In M. W. McLaughlin and D. C. Philips (eds.), *Evaluation and Education: At Quarter Century. Ninetieth Yearbook of the National Society for the Study of Education, Part II.* Chicago: University of Chicago Press, 1991.

Stake, R. E. "Case Studies." In N. K. Denzin and Y. S. Lincoln (eds.), *Handbook of Qualitative Research.* Thousand Oaks, Calif.: Sage, 1994.

Stake, R. E. "The Fleeting Discernment of Quality." In L. Mabry (ed.), *Evaluation and the Post-Modern Dilemma: Advances in Program Evaluation.* Series Editor, R. Stake. Greenwich, Conn.: JAI Press, 1997a.

Stake, R. E. "Advocacy in Evaluation: A Necessary Evil?" In E. Chelimsky and W. R. Shadish (eds.) *Evaluation for the Twenty-First Century.* Thousand Oaks, Calif.: Sage, 1997b.

Stake, R. E., Bresler, L., and Mabry L. (eds.). *Custom and Cherishing: The Arts in Elementary Schools, Studies of U.S. Elementary Schools Protraying the Ordinary Problems of Teachers Teaching Music, Drama, Dance, and the Visual Arts in 1987–1990.* Urbana-Champaign: Council for Research in Music Education, University of Illinois, 1991.

Stake, R., DeStefano, L., Harnisch , D., Sloane, K., and Davis, R. *Evaluation of the National Youth Sports Program.* Report prepared for the National Collegiate Athletic Association. Champaign: CIRCE, University of Illinois, 1997.

Stake, R. E., and Kerr, D. "René Magritte, Constructivism, and the Researcher as Interpreter." *Educational Theory,* 1994, 45(1), 55–61.

Stake, R. E., and Mabry, L. "Case Study for a Deep Understanding of Teaching." In A. C. Omstein (ed.), *Teaching: Theory into Practice.* Boston: Allyn & Bacon, 1995.

Stake, R., Raths, J., St. John, M., Trumbull, D., Jenness, D., Foster, M., Sullivan, S., Denny, T., and Easley, J. *Teacher Preparation Archives: Case Studies of MSF-Funded Middle School Science and Mathematics Teacher Preparation Projects.* Champaign: CIRCE, University of Illinois, 1993.

Stake, R., Souchet, T., Clift, R., Mabry, L., Basi, M., Whiteaker, M., Mills, C., and Dunbar, T. *School Improvement: Facilitating Professional Development in Chicago School Reform.* Champaign: CIRCE, University of Illinois, 1996.

Stake, R. E., and Trumbull, D. J. "Naturalistic Generalizations." *Review Journal of Philosophy and Social Science,* 1982, 7(1–2), 1–12.

Tyler, R. W. *Basic Principles of Curriculum and Instruction.* Chicago: University of Chicago Press, 1950.

TINEKE A. ABMA is working at the Department of Health Care Policy and Management of the Erasmus University, Rotterdam, The Netherlands.

ROBERT E. STAKE is professor of educational psychology at the University of Illinois, Urbana-Champaign, and director of CIRCE.

2

In the 1970s Stake offered a rationale for representing the perspectives of stakeholders, which was liberating and highly influential, though his insistence that evaluative claims are subjective left responsive evaluators in an arbitrary posture.

Responsive Evaluation (and Its Influence on Deliberative Democratic Evaluation)

Ernest R. House

In the late 1960s and early 1970s the dominant approach to evaluation was to carefully develop in advance the designs for evaluating programs. This approach was inspired by Campbell and Stanley's (1963) strong influence. Although evaluation studies seldom achieved the rigor advocated, evaluators aspired to be scientific, and that meant strong experimental design and quantitative measurement focused on outcomes.

For those working at the Center for Instructional Research and Curriculum Evaluation (CIRCE) at the University of Illinois, these admonitions seemed inadequate. I was conducting a four-year evaluation of the Illinois Program for Gifted Youth. This study was formulated on Stake's earlier data matrix that divided information to be collected into description and judgment, with each of those categories crossed by antecedents, transactions, and outcomes (Stake, 1967). Although we found no way to employ randomized designs in evaluating the hundreds of gifted education programs in the state, we spent considerable resources attempting to measure program dimensions rigorously. We later published these findings in research journals, which accepted only quantitative studies in those days.

At the end of four years I realized that we could have provided essentially the same information to the state legislature within one year and for a fraction of the cost if we had asked people their judgments about the programs, though such information would lack scientific credibility by the standards of the day. I also recognized that the only way we could make sense of the thirty kinds of data we had collected about each local program was

NEW DIRECTIONS FOR EVALUATION, no. 92, Winter 2001   © John Wiley & Sons, Inc.

to construct narratives that interpreted this information. The diverse pieces of data were not interpretable without some framework. Yet there was little guidance about constructing such narratives in the literature, other than vague references to applying social science theory.

In our next ventures, we conducted evaluations by interviewing stake-holders, sometimes more and sometimes less rigorously, and writing up these interview findings and observations in interpretive narratives—case studies. There was no theoretical rationale for such a practice. The practice preceded the theory. Bob Stake, associate director of CIRCE, provided such a rationale under the rubric of "responsive evaluation," capturing some of the reasoning that led us into such an enterprise.

Stake ([1972] 1975) contrasted the responsiveness of his approach to the "pre-ordinate" designs presented in statistics texts. According to Stake, the evaluator should approach a program without preconceived notions of the shape the study should take. Only after inspecting the program should the evaluator formulate the evaluation design. Although Stake did not insist, these responsive studies took the form of qualitative case studies. Later, he said quantitative studies could be responsive, while admitting almost none were. Responsive evaluation became case study evaluation, though there were other approaches to doing case studies.

For those of us conducting evaluations, having an explicit rationale was liberating. For most studies, evaluators have to produce a written proposal. Employing terms like "responsive" and "pre-ordinate" legitimated our efforts. These words sounded more professional than saying we were going to talk to people in and around the program and write up a report. Indeed, pre-ordinate proponents had the advantage of proclaiming the virtues of rigorous preset designs in their proposals, arguing that having "X's" and "O's" in the right places captured reality somehow. We needed a legitimating rationale. As Stake elaborated his approach, we gleaned additional ideas as to what we might do in such studies, though detailed procedures were never the focus of responsive evaluation. The theoretical informed the practical, just as the practical had informed the theoretical.

Although such a development may seem strange, I suspect it is typical of new approaches. Evaluators were doing something resembling program theory before theorists explicated such positions in the literature. Now many evaluators justify their studies on the basis of program theory rationales. From aberrant practice to new theory back to legitimated practice seems to be the course of events. And it is not a bad course of development since it tethers theory to the ground to some degree.

Features of Responsive Evaluation

In Stake's view, evaluations are "responsive" if they orient to program activities, respond to audience requirements for information, and refer to different value perspectives in reporting the successes and failures of the program

(Stake, [1972] 1975). But this formulation is too brief to distinguish Stake's work from other approaches. One must look deeper into the orientation, beliefs, and assumptions the evaluator brings to the task to distinguish responsive evaluation.

For Stake, there is no single true value to anything. Value lies in the eye of the beholder, which means that there might be many valid interpretations of the same events, depending on a person's point of view, interests, and beliefs. And there might be many valid evaluations of the same program, some of which contradict each other. The task of the evaluator is to collect the views of people in and around the program, the stakeholders, and possibly views beyond the stakeholders.

These diverse views should be represented in the evaluation report, both to do honor to the stakeholders (honor is a traditional virtue for Stake) and so that readers of the report can draw their own conclusions about the program. Value pluralism applies to audiences of the evaluation as well as to stakeholders. This set of beliefs is a variation of value relativism—no impartial or objective value judgments are possible. (*Impartial* is a better term, as *objective* carries with it other meanings, but the objective-subjective pairing has been used most often in the past.)

As Stake developed his rationale more than thirty years ago, I asked him where his ideas came from. He showed me a pamphlet, *Perception: A Transactional Approach* (1954) by Ittelson and Cantril, both from Princeton, where Stake had done his Ph.D. Here is a quote:

> There are three features of perception which deserve special attention with respect to human perception. First, the facts of perception always present themselves through concrete individuals dealing with concrete situations. They can be studied only in terms of the *transactions* in which they can be observed. Second, within such transactions, perceiving is always done by a particular person from his own unique position space and time and with his own combination of experiences and needs. Perception always enters into the transaction from the unique *personal behavioral center* of the perceiving individual. And, third, within the particular transaction and operating from his own personal behavioral center, each of us, through perceiving, creates for himself his own psychological environment by attributing certain aspects of his experience to an environment which he believes exists independent of the experience. This characteristic of perception we can label *externalization* [Ittelson and Cantril, 1954, p. 2].

Knowledge for Stake is situational. That is, knowledge is about concrete events in particular settings. Knowledge is context bound. The evaluator must get close to local events in context to understand them. To understand a program one must travel into the program setting in the deeper sense to see where people live and how they think. Their beliefs and judgments should be included in the report even if the evaluator does not agree with them, perhaps especially if the evaluator disagrees. In-depth investigation and reporting honors program participants and gives readers the information to draw their own conclusions. Respect for the local setting and the people striving within it is a central value.

The method par excellence for investigating and representing the beliefs and values of stakeholders in context is the case study. "[M]ost case studies feature: descriptions that are complex, holistic, and involving a myriad of not highly isolated variables; data that are likely to be gathered at least partly by personalistic observation; and a writing style that is informal, perhaps narrative, possibly with verbatim quotation, illustration, and even allusion and metaphor. Comparisons are implicit rather than explicit" (Stake, 1978, p. 7). In Stake's view, much of the knowledge conveyed in case studies is tacit, in contrast to propositional knowledge. Readers experience the program vicariously through reading the case. This interest in qualitative case study techniques led Stake into aesthetic considerations, sometimes into an "auteur" posture for the evaluator where the writing became paramount.

Since the evaluator relies on impressions and "personalistic" observations and not on standard data collection and analysis techniques, how does one keep from being wrong? The major way is to try out the ideas on people in the setting. Let them respond to what the evaluator has written and challenge it. If others disagree, the ideas need to be reexamined. However, in checking with people, there is no participation of stakeholders the way participatory theorists would have it. Stake is firmly opposed to stakeholder participation. The evaluation study is the job of the evaluator, and the evaluator remains in control of all aspects. What goes into the report and what the evaluator responds to is at the discretion of the evaluator. Others can disagree if they like.

A further safeguard against error is for the evaluator to state conclusions tentatively, allowing others freedom to disagree, even encouraging them to do so. Evaluators should admit their fallibility and make this known to stakeholders and audiences. After all, the readers' opinion is as good as the evaluator's.

These beliefs reflect both Stake's training and his small-town Nebraska background. He distrusts central authority, which presumes to impose its will on local people, wrongly and mistakenly. He distrusts grand theories, like philosophic and social science theories, which are too imperial. Theories drown out local knowledge, which is more relevant. He distrusts social movements, which lead people astray against their better interests. His values are individualist, populist, and Midwestern, sometimes including righteousness in defense of these values. And he incorporated these ideas into his evaluation theory.

In blending the professional and personal Stake is no different from other major evaluation theorists. Virtually all of them incorporate ideas, beliefs, and values derived from their backgrounds and personal experience.

The major theorists are major theorists because they have been able to transform their beliefs, values, and experiences into concepts that are persuasive to large numbers of people. Their theories and personalities blend together, one reason why critics of their ideas are often surprised by the vehemence with which the ideas are defended. My interpretation of these influences on Stake's work is consistent with his view that ideas come from the concrete and personal.

Stake's ideas influenced my own work in several ways. First, he demonstrated there could be different approaches to conducting studies, as opposed to the orthodoxy of the time. And he was tolerant of other approaches as well. He endorsed innovation in the field. Second, he provided a formidable rationale for why qualitative studies might be useful and legitimated the use of case studies. Third, he featured stakeholder perspectives as integral elements in evaluations. And he stressed the critical importance of context in understanding local actions.

There were also substantial differences between us. He stressed that his approach was fittingly subjective. I saw the need for objective approaches. Further, coming from an industrial working class background, I saw a need for social justice in evaluation. Rather than reject grand theories, I looked not only to my experience but to philosophy and political science as sources—Rawls's theory of justice, Habermas's communication theory, Perelman and Olbrechts-Tyteca's new rhetoric, Bhaskar's realism, and so forth.

In the mid-1970s when I developed a taxonomy of evaluation approaches and their underlying assumptions, I put Stake's work in the subjectivist ethics, intuitionist-pluralist category, which included transactional knowing and a subjectivist epistemology (House, 1980, p. 48). By contrast, the alternative taxonomy branch that included objectivist ethics had no representative approaches at all. My colleague Barry MacDonald said, "You will fill in the blank with your own approach eventually." It took a while to fill the objectivist ethics and epistemology category with deliberative democratic evaluation (House and Howe, 1999). My position built on some of Stake's ideas but journeyed a long ways from them.

Responsive Evaluation in Perspective

The great strength of responsive evaluation is that it helped break the intellectual stranglehold that single-method approaches had on evaluation at one time. It legitimated different avenues to conducting evaluations. This influence was liberating and highly beneficial as evaluation evolved into a multimethod professional practice. Stake's responsive evaluation played a major role in expanding the field intellectually.

Furthermore, respect and concern for those evaluated—honoring, attending to, and representing their perspectives—was a sorely needed change from the subject mentality that has been common in the human sciences. Stake encouraged evaluators to look away from the statistics texts and toward those people whose programs were under review. Evaluation took on concrete, real-life characters. Such change was enlightening and the right thing to do.

The weakness of responsive evaluation is that it can be conservative and relativistic. Shadish, Cook, and Leviton call Stake's incremental, evolutionary concept of change conservative: "Stake bites the hand that feeds us, arguing that federal and state influence is too great, has disenfranchised local stakeholders, and has discouraged them from solving their own problems" (1991, p. 296). Stake accepts this conservatism label: "I don't want evaluation to be closely identified with revolutionary change or even with evolutionary change, as opposed to protecting what is good, arresting deterioration" (Stake and Abma, 1994). And he believes things are deteriorating, compared to the way they used to be.

He is prepared to honor and defend the status quo and has argued that evaluation should not change power relationships among people. The power structure should be the same after the evaluation as before. "In my reports I am very likely to tell of much that is good. My colleagues who are left-wingers are less likely, I believe, to report that goodness. They often paint a picture of abomination that will arouse folks to work harder to alleviate these things" (Stake and Abma, 1994). There is, however, a potential inconsistency between not wanting power relationships to change as a result of an evaluation and letting people draw their own conclusions from the evaluation. After all, on reading the report readers might want the power relationships to change.

A deeper problem is that responsive evaluation can be relativistic and arbitrary. If value claims, including evaluative conclusions, depend on the person making them and no claim is better than any other, where does that leave us? Are not all claims equal? How can various claims be resolved if this is so? There is a contradiction between evaluation and relativism. If all claims are equally valid and depend on a person's background, beliefs, and interests, how can evaluators draw conclusions legitimately? What authority do evaluators have to do so since anyone else's opinion is just as valid?

Stake's answer seems to be that ultimately the evaluator decides, which must mean that judgment is dependent on the evaluator's values and personality. "Needs are regularly what someone else thinks the needy lack. But which of us does not see something we badly want as a need? And if evaluators are not ready to let the needy define their own needs, where is the democratic ethic? The resolution for evaluators is to hear the pleas, to deliberate, sometimes to negotiate, but regularly, non-democratically, to decide what their interests are" (Stake, 2000, p. 104). One way to resolve issues in a relativistic world is to have an arbiter.

In responsive evaluation the evaluator assumes the arbiter role, even while allowing that others might legitimately come to other conclusions. Stakeholders themselves are banned from participating. And here Stake senses a contradiction in himself. He admits the same issues arise repeatedly in his work and these issues are not derived from stakeholders. "Some issues are just deep within me" (Stake and Abma, 1994). He is honest enough to admit that basing issues on his personality and not on responding to stakeholders is contrary to his stated position: "There is more rigidity in my work than the responsive flexibility I am presenting" (Stake and Abma, 1994).

At some level I think these contradictions arise from accepting the fact-value dichotomy. Facts are one thing and values something else. Facts can be resolved empirically but values cannot be since they depend on the beholder. Anyone's value claims, including evaluative conclusions, are as valid as anyone else's. There can be impartial factual claims (perhaps) but there cannot be impartial value claims. Accepting the fact-value dichotomy poses a conundrum. Value claims, including evaluative conclusions, cannot be justified.

I believe the solution lies in rejecting relativism and the fact-value dichotomy altogether. Value claims are not necessarily relative. Some value claims can be justified impartially, especially those value claims that we call evaluative conclusions. Just as factual claims can be justified by using professional procedures for collecting and analyzing data, so too value claims might be justified by using other procedures. Actually, fact and value claims fuse together in evaluative conclusions. The solution involves discovering or inventing appropriate procedures for drawing impartial evaluative conclusions.

Stake always saw such claims as subjective—anyone's opinion is as good as anyone else's—a legacy perhaps of transactional knowing, honoring local people, and accepting the fact-value dichotomy. By contrast, my view of arriving at evaluative conclusions is by processing stakeholder views more systematically. In other words, take stakeholder views seriously but not at face value. Weigh them against other views and information. Subject them to dialogue and deliberation procedures as rational tests of their validity. Where might we find such procedures? We might look where value conflicts have been resolved most successfully—in democratic institutions—and add these procedures to our repertoire of traditional methods.

When Lee Cronbach introduced my talk at Stake's retirement conference in 1998, he said these deliberative democratic ideas were familiar to him. They were Deweyan efforts at discussing and solving public problems. In the 1940s Cronbach and Tom Hastings, the founder of CIRCE, came to Urbana from Chicago, where they had been imbued with Dewey's ideas. The transactional knowing concept was derived from Dewey (Dewey and Bentley, 1949), though the psychologists Ittelson, Cantril, and Stake gave it a more subjective, individualistic interpretation.

There was also a public aspect to Dewey. Although people interpreted the world transactionally through their experience, their experience was shaped largely by the social world. Hence, much of the content of their world was social, public, and shared by others. It was learned, not invented, by people. Consequently, the path to social change was to discuss and deliberate on the content that affected public problems. In that sense evaluation can be democratic and impartial (objective) in ethics and epistemology.

References

Campbell, D. T., and Stanley, J. C. *Experimental and Quasi-Experimental Designs for Research*. Chicago: Rand McNally, 1963.

Dewey, J., and Bentley, A. F. *Knowing and the Known*. Boston: Beacon Press, 1949.

House, E. R. *Evaluating with Validity*. Thousand Oaks, Calif.: Sage, 1980.

House, E. R., and Howe, K. R. *Values in Evaluation and Social Research*. Thousand Oaks, Calif.: Sage, 1999.

Ittelson, W. H., and Cantril, H. *Perception: A Transactional Approach*. Garden City, N.Y.: Doubleday, 1954.

Shadish, W. R., Jr., Cook, T. D., and Leviton, L. C. *Foundations of Program Evaluation: Theories of Practice*. Thousand Oaks, Calif.: Sage, 1991.

Stake, R. E. "The Countenance of Educational Evaluation." *Teachers College Record*, 1967, 68(7), 523–540.

Stake, R. E. "Responsive Evaluation." Mimeo report. Urbana-Champaign: University of Illinois, 1972. Revised as "To Evaluate an Arts Program." In R. E. Stake (ed.), *Evaluating the Arts in Education: A Responsive Approach*. Columbus, Ohio: Merrill, 1975.

Stake, R. E. "The Case Study Method in Social Inquiry." *Educational Researcher*, 1978, 7, 5–8.

Stake, R. E. "A Modest Commitment to the Promotion of Democracy." In K. E. Ryan and L. DeStefano (eds.), *Evaluation as a Democratic Process: Promoting Inclusion, Dialogue, and Deliberation*. New Directions for Evaluation, no. 85. San Francisco: Jossey-Bass, 2000.

Stake, R. E., and Abma, T. A. "Interview Notes." Unpublished, 1994.

ERNEST R. HOUSE is professor of education at the University of Colorado, Boulder. He can be reached at ernie.house@colorado.edu.

3

The essential place of race and culture in the meanings of responsive evaluation are argued through (1) a historical accounting of the significant but inexplicably unknown contributions of early African American evaluators and (2) the unassailable warrant for contemporary responsiveness to our "long silenced cultures of color."

Nobody Knows My Name: In Praise of African American Evaluators Who Were Responsive

Stafford Hood

Recent evaluative models and approaches by Greene (1997), Fetterman (1994), and Patton (1994) appear to be open to the central importance of culture when evaluators work with and within communities of color. For me, the first ray of light on the relevance of culture for educational evaluation appeared in Stake's ([1973] 1987) paper on responsive evaluation. After Wilcox (1984) and Chevalier, Roark-Calnek, and Strahan (1982) found responsive evaluation to be a viable and appropriate framework for evaluating programs in the highly complex context of Native American cultures, I wrote about the relevance of culture for test construction (Hood and Parker, 1989). Further encouragement came from a noted African American evaluator who argued that responsive evaluation was an approach that accepted culturally diverse factors as being central to an evaluation (Madison, 1992). Herein, I revisit Stake's work because I have personally benefited from it and from my interactions with him and others who have called the Center for Instructional Research and Curriculum Evaluation (CIRCE) home.

Other encouraging signs regarding the relevance of culture for educational evaluation and the need for a more racially diverse educational evaluation community continue to appear. Conversations among Stanfield (1999), House (1999), Patton (1999), and Hopson (1999) in the *American*

The author expresses his deepest appreciation to Mrs. Leander Boykin (Tallahassee, Florida) for providing invaluable insights about Dr. Boykin, his work, and his experiences.

Journal of Evaluation on the relevance of race and culture in evaluation have been accompanied by preliminary but meaningful efforts within the American Evaluation Association (AEA). The Kellogg-funded Building Diversity Initiative and the recent establishment of the Diversity Committee as an AEA standing committee appear to be steps in the right direction.

The Kellogg-funded initiative seeks to "improve the quality and effectiveness of evaluation by increasing the number of racially and ethnically diverse evaluators in the evaluation profession and improving the capacity of evaluators to work across cultures" (American Evaluation Association, 2000). The purpose of the AEA Committee is to "Increase the diversity of the members and leaders in the AEA and to provide leadership within AEA and outside of AEA to address this issue" (American Evaluation Association, 1998). Such efforts are timely, long overdue, and essential. The astute observation that "the challenge facing America in [this new] century will be the shaping, at long last, of a truly common public culture, one responsive to the long silenced cultures of color" (Gates, 1991, p. 712, as cited in Greene, 1993, p. 13) is apparently finding receptive hearts within the educational evaluation community.

Notwithstanding these encouraging trends, there was an empty spot within me when I first ruminated about my African American perspective on educational evaluation. Who has gone before me? Where is our history?

The first purpose of this chapter is to remedy our collective ignorance about scholarly work in educational evaluation by African Americans during the influential Tyler Years (1940–1960), much of which was importantly responsive. During these years, Ralph Tyler championed evaluation as assessing the fulfillment of program goals and objectives. This chapter thus recovers some of our important history as evaluators—yet it is merely a starting point for further discussions about the need for an African American perspective in evaluation theory and practice. The second purpose of the chapter is to reflect on what it means to be responsive in contemporary evaluation practice. I recall wondering during my first assignment as an educational evaluator: Am I being faithful to what a responsive evaluator should and should not do, as defined by Stake? and Does my "lived experience" as an African American better equip me to be a responsive evaluator in the African American community? I remain uncertain about the answer to the first question because I still have difficulty maintaining impartiality when evaluating programs that primarily serve poor and racial minorities (particularly African Americans). However, I soon learned that I was indeed able to respond to the needs of the African American community because of my lived experience within that community.

At the present time, for me as an African American evaluator, to be responsive fundamentally means to attend substantively and politically to issues of culture and race in evaluation practice. The principal contribution of this chapter is its demonstration that, in the early years of educational evaluation, there *were* trained African American scholars who conducted educational evaluations and published in scholarly journals—yet went unnoticed. I further argue that the increased participation of African Americans and other evaluators of color is a pragmatic necessity for evaluation, as well as a sensible and morally decent thing to do. The reader is advised that my view enlarges the present boundaries of responsive evaluation. For this, I ask your thoughtful consideration—but offer no apology. As an African American man I neither seek nor expect affirmation in a field that has only recently included white women in its pantheon.

African American Scholars in the Tyler Years

Until the late 1990s I was unable to name a single African American scholar who had contributed to the educational evaluation literature during the Tyler Years (1940–1960). The Tyler Years spanned the period of World War II, desegregation of the Armed Services, the GI Bill, the Korean War, and *Brown v. Board of Education of Topeka* (1954). All had major impact on the African American community by increasing access to educational opportunities. The Tyler Years witnessed legal struggles that challenged the separate but unequal education of African Americans. Consequently, it seemed odd to me that African Americans had not pursued educational evaluation as an area of scholarly inquiry. It was particularly frustrating to ask prominent and learned members of the evaluation community about their knowledge of the contributions of African American during the Tyler Years and what I term the "reconstruction" period of educational evaluation (1960 to 1975). My question produced one of two responses: "There were none" or "I don't know of any." As an African American who happens to be an evaluator, I have searched for an African American history in educational evaluation, in part motivated by "the experiences of pain and abandonment [that] have led to a search for roots and on occasion, for a revision of recorded history" (Greene, 1993, p. 17).

I began my search with the assumption that those who pursued evaluative inquiry within their dissertation research were likely candidates for publishing scholarly works in this area. Anderson's (1984) historical study, "Toward a History and Bibliography of the Afro-American Doctorate and Professoriate in Education, 1896 to 1980" includes a bibliography of African American dissertations (261) in education between 1925 and 1951. Charles Thompson (founding editor of the *Journal of Negro Education*, Howard University, 1932) was the first African American to receive a doctorate in Education (Ph.D., University of Chicago, 1925), two years prior to Ralph Tyler's doctorate from the same institution. My review focused on dissertations with titles that included "evaluation" or descriptors that were used synonymously with evaluation (for example, appraisal, accreditation, critical analysis). My subsequent review of the actual dissertations or journal publications that were drawn from dissertation research yielded a list of twenty-five African American doctoral recipients. The earliest dissertation by an

African American to include the word "evaluation" in its title was by Edward L. Washington (1935, New York University) and the first by an African American woman was by Rose Browne (1939, Harvard University).

An author search of the twenty-five names on the list, using the Periodicals Content Index's (PCI) electronic database of 11 million journal articles in 3,450 humanities and social science journals for the period 1770 to 1993, produced no publications by ten of the individuals on this list of twenty-five. However, fifteen had indeed published work in scholarly journals and ten had published large-scale evaluation studies, smaller studies, or scholarly discussions of evaluation theory and practice. Although, the primary outlets for their work were the *Journal of Negro Education* and the *Negro Educational Review,* they also published in so-called mainstream educational journals (for example, *Journal of Educational Research, Educational Administration and Supervision,* and *School and Society*). While it is clear that African Americans *were* publishing work in the area of educational evaluation during the period from 1938 through 1960, their work has not been cited as being a part of the mainstream evaluation literature in our reading lists for courses on program evaluation. I find it curious that African American evaluators went unnoticed when a number of them had received their degrees from prestigious public and private universities with reputations not only for their educational research but also for the emerging field of educational evaluation. Two examples illustrate my point.

Ohio State University (OSU) was the first notable center devoted to the examination of evaluative theory, research and practice, due to the influence of Ralph Tyler. Tyler was a professor of education at OSU from 1929 to 1938, where he also initiated the Eight Year Study for the Progressive Association, and was joined in his efforts by Lee Cronbach and Benjamin Bloom (O'Shea, 1985). When Tyler joined the faculty at the University of Chicago as chair of its Department of Education in 1938 (he would remain there until 1953), he moved the Eight Year Study with him (O'Shea, 1985). Concurrently, Greene's (1946) research identifies Reid E. Jackson as the fourth African American to receive a doctorate in education from OSU. Jackson's dissertation, "A Critical Analysis of Curricula for Educating Secondary School Teachers in Negro Colleges of Alabama" (Ph.D., 1938), clearly employs a Tylerian "objectives oriented" approach for his evaluative study. It is highly probable that Jackson, as one of four African doctoral students in education at OSU in the mid-1930s (Greene, 1946) would have come in contact with Tyler and others working on the Eight Year Study, since his dissertation employed the same evaluative methodology found in the project reports. A similar question can be raised in the case of Aaron Brown, who, six years later, was the third African American to receive his doctorate in education from the University of Chicago. His dissertation, "An Evaluation of the Accredited Secondary Schools for Negroes in the South" (Ph.D., 1944), was Tylerian at base. In the case of Brown, the oversight is more disturbing. Brown's work was not cited within the context of educational evaluation, although Tyler was the chair of the University of Chicago's Department of Education when Brown received his degree.

Since both Jackson and Brown received their doctorates from premier centers for training in evaluation, it seems improbable that they would have been unknown to the major figures in the evaluation community at the time. This is troubling to me. Greene (1993) has said it well: "There is really nothing more to say—except why. But since why is difficult to handle, one must take refuge in how" (p. 16). Because, in the case under consideration the *why* may be a distasteful and unproductive conversation, it may be more desirable to focus on the *how* and thereby come to appreciate the contributions of early African American evaluators to educational evaluation theory and practice.

Race is the foremost social issue of our generation and has been since the inception of our nation. For the matter at hand, I aver that race influences who is awarded evaluation contracts, who is awarded professorial positions, and who is listened to by evaluation clients. The chapter now turns to responsive evaluation as a framework for understanding and appreciating the relevance of the early work of African American evaluators.

Responsive Evaluation and the Early African American Evaluators

Stake's description (1973) of the structure of responsive evaluation and the evaluator's role within it provides a lens for viewing the work of early African American evaluators. I would argue that the "shared lived experiences" of African Americans in education during the Tyler Years morally *required* them to be responsive evaluators. More about that later. First, since responsive evaluation evolved from Stake's countenance article (1967), I shall begin with that seminal work.

The Inclusion of Qualitative Data Stake's countenance article called for evaluators to consider a broader range of data beyond the quantitatively driven focus of the Tyler model and was groundbreaking in the reconstruction period of evaluation that began in the 1960s. The countenance approach emphasized that a rich description of the program and the context in which it functioned were critical to achieving something more than a superficial understanding of the program. The message seemed clear that qualitative data—observations, interviews, document reviews—could and should have equal importance as quantitative data in the evaluation of a program. In the case of programs that serve racial minorities, it is extremely difficult, when possible at all, to explain cultural context and to interpret outcomes without the use of qualitative information. An unheralded African American evaluator during the same era anticipated Stake's view of the importance of qualitative data in evaluating educational programs.

Leander Boykin was the first African American to receive a Ph.D. in education from Stanford University (in 1948) and did postdoctoral work at

Harvard University in 1957–58. In one of several works on evaluation, Boykin provided a set of ten "guiding principles, characteristics, and functions of effective evaluation" (Boykin, 1957). One point specifically addressed the importance of gathering quantitative and qualitative data for evaluation: "Such newer techniques as anecdotal records, observational methods . . . personal reports, projective methods, sociometric methods, case studies, and cumulative records are required to assess such objectives as knowledge and understandings, skills, interests, aptitudes, attitudes, personal social adjustment, critical thinking, and health and physical development. . . . [Additionally] techniques are needed to evaluate such correlative factors as the social and economic backgrounds of pupils and the educational climate in which classroom and school activities are conducted" (Boykin, 1957, p. 118).

Other early African American educational evaluators subscribed to the use of qualitative data in their large-scale evaluation studies of accreditation of segregated secondary schools (Brown, 1944), HBCU curricula (Oak, 1938) and state educational systems (Brown, 1947; Jackson 1940a, 1940b). These early African American evaluators collected qualitative and quantitative data to reveal differences in the educational experiences of African Americans and Caucasian Americans. Insightfully, they concurred that there were limitations in the application of quantitative data. Jackson (1940a) protested vehemently that "the impersonal criterion offered in the computation of an arithmetical ratio deriving from population count does not suffice" (p. 59). Boykin (1950) concluded that "quantitative differences between white and Negro education, important as they are, cannot and do not explain the whole of the problem. Certain historical and other factors must also be taken into account" (p. 535). These statements show that from an African American perspective, for over a half century, evaluative inquiry based on quantitative analysis alone has been recognized as "impersonal" and insufficient in the context of African American education.

These African American evaluators were thus responding to the evaluation needs of their communities. It was their *response* to the pursuit of a fuller understanding of educational programs that strongly resonated with my thinking about program evaluation—particularly for those programs primarily serving racial minority groups in general and African Americans in particular.

The Importance of Shared Lived Experience. In 1940 Brown raised an issue that is still with us sixty years later, when he wrote that African Americans have "special and critical needs growing out of differences in background and existing conditions. . . . [The question is] what special considerations, if any, should be made in the evaluation of schools for [African Americans]" (Brown, 1944, p. 498). Responsive evaluation may provide a framework for considering these "special considerations" in evaluating African American education. Similarly, any consideration of the issues and concerns of the African American experience in the educational system during the period of 1940 to 1960 must consider their overall inequitable treatment grounded in overt and covert racism.

Given the dramatically different histories of African Americans and Caucasian Americans within the American educational system, African Americans who engaged in evaluation would see the educational system from a different perspective than would Caucasian Americans. Anderson (1988), Dubois (1932, 1935), and Thompson (1947, 1955) have demonstrated that the history of African Americans in American education before, during, and after slavery has been a rich and troubled one that continues today. Anderson provides a perspective of "the education of blacks in the South" covering the period of 1860 to 1935. His cogent analysis applies equally well to the 1940s, 1950s and early 1960s. He stated: "A careful examination of blacks' enduring beliefs in education and their historic struggle to acquire decent educational opportunities against almost overwhelming odds leaves little room to attribute their relatively low levels of educational attainment to uncongenial cultural values or educational norms. That more was not achieved means little, for the conditions have been appallingly difficult. Cultural values were hardly relevant in a society in which opportunities for education were unavailable" (Anderson, 1984, p. 285).

Much of Anderson's analysis is arguably relevant today. The view that African Americans' cultural values are a major impediment for their acquisition of "decent educational opportunities" has persisted in spite of the lack of convincing evidence to support such a claim. What we need are more informed interpretations of cultural values. Allow me to put it rhetorically. Is it not more likely that those who have a shared lived experience within the context under evaluation can more accurately provide a critical analysis and evaluation of African American education? Who stands the better chance of responding to the contextual imperatives of "black folks"? Whose counsel will be more heeded? (Rhetoric, while perhaps lacking justification for some white readers, well connects to culture. It embodies our use of call and response in our music, our church service, and our informal social discourse. The writer must pick his audience.)

A major priority of responsive evaluation's structure should be to provide the audience of the evaluation with a "vicarious experience" as a substitute for a "direct experience" so that the audience better understands what the program is like (Stake, [1973] 1987). The culturally responsive evaluator orchestrates an evaluation that culminates in a reporting of findings that comes closest to letting the audience see, hear, and touch the essence of the program and how it is functioning. I have argued earlier that a shared lived experience (Hood, 1998) could and possibly should be accepted as being important and valuable in the evaluation of programs serving members of racial minority groups. Evaluators of color are more likely to have "direct experiences" with their own racial and cultural group that may inform their evaluation of programs serving this group. Consequently, this may enhance their ability to provide the audience with a "vicarious experience" that comes closest to a "direct experience." The framework for guiding the evaluator's efforts to produce such a vicarious experience resides within the substantive structure of responsive evaluation.

Issues and the Structure of Responsive Evaluation. The substantive structure of responsive evaluation can be seen to include four major assumptions:

- Issues are the "advanced organizers" for evaluation study instead of objectives or hypotheses.
- Issues are the structure for continuing discussions and data gathering plan.
- Human observers are best instruments.
- Evaluators should get their information in sufficient amounts from numerous independent and credible sources so that it effectively represents the perceived status of the program, however complex (Stake, [1973] 1987).

It is important to note that for two of these assumptions, issues provide the framework for the structural component. The evaluative work of African American evaluators during the 1940s and 1950s could clearly be viewed as being focused on the major issues that were facing the African American community during this period. Jackson (1940a) framed the "advanced organizers" in evaluating African American education by indicating that "the needs of the group, individually, and collectively, must serve as a criterion if a true democracy is to be achieved" (Jackson, 1940a, p. 59).

At the time of Jackson's remarks "separate but equal" was the law of the land and its impact on the African American community was oppressive. It permeated the total experience of the community since community survival was inextricably linked to the educational experiences of its members. Separate and dramatically unequal education of African Americans (K–12 and postsecondary) served as the focus for issues and the primary organizer of evaluative inquiry and practice by African American evaluators. After a lengthy analysis of data and studies by others reported in a special issue of the *Journal of Negro Education* on segregated schools in seventeen southern states and the District of Columbia, Thompson stated: "One of the most important and inevitable conclusions is that Negroes in the separate school systems of the 17 states and the District of Columbia which require racial segregation have been the victims of gross discrimination in the provision of educational opportunities. On the whole Negroes have had only about one-fourth the educational opportunity afforded to whites in the same school systems (1947, pp. 264–265).

Thompson described the inadequate production of African American professionals to meet the needs of the African American community. In a series of compelling examples, Thompson (1947) reported that in 1939–40 medical schools enrolled one white medical student for every 4,781 white Americans, one law student for every 3,267, and one dental student for every 15,930. At the same time, there was one African American medical student for every 20,298 African Americans, one law student for every 25,372, and one dental student for every 33,830. Further, there was one white engineer to every 644 of the white population and one Negro engineer to every 130,700 of the Negro population—proportionately 202 times as many white engineers as Negro.

In my view it would have been socially irresponsible for African Americans trained in evaluation techniques to engage in evaluative efforts that did not address the unequal educational opportunities and resources that were implicit in many northern states and explicit in the southern ones. A pattern existed in the evaluative practice of these early African American evaluators. They focused on aggregated looks at inequities in segregated schools and colleges for African Americans in the South across the southern states as well as in individual southern states. For example, Brown (1944) evaluated accredited secondary schools for Negroes in the South and also looked at the elementary, secondary, and postsecondary experience of Negroes in Georgia (Brown, 1947). Boykin's broad look across the southern states addressed the differentials in financial resources (1950), teacher salaries (1949), and the interpretation of quantitative data for segregated schools (1954). Boykin also conducted an evaluative study on Louisiana's public Negro higher education institutions (1962). These were the issues that served as their "advanced organizers" and addressed the second point in the substantive structure of responsive evaluation.

The third assumption of responsive evaluation's substantive structure indicates that "human observers" are the best. These African American evaluators were "human observers" who had a "shared lived experience" in the African American community that allowed them not only to make observations but to understand the meaning of what had been observed (Hood, 1998). Similarly, those within today's African American community are often discouraged by the tasks of educating and translating for evaluators without the necessary lived experience. I would further argue that comparably trained white evaluators would not have been received as readily within the schools, universities, and communities as were these African American evaluators. Consequently, these early African American evaluators were more likely to receive more cooperation and honest responses from African American stakeholders that would facilitate their access to pertinent information and validation regarding the accuracy of their findings. We may wish the world were otherwise, but race matters in the settings of the disenfranchised. It was so then; it is so now. I acknowledge and celebrate the rich cultural diversity within my African American community, for which no one person can speak. But all of us can speak from *within* the community.

The final assumption of responsive evaluation's substantive structure addresses the evaluator's need to collect information from multiple independent and credible sources to effectively represent the program's present status (Stake, [1973] 1987). Boykin (1957) prophetically saw the importance of including the perspectives of multiple program stakeholders in conducting an evaluation. One of his ten guiding principles, characteristics, and functions of an effective evaluation asserted: "[Evaluation] is a cooperative process involving pupils, parents, teachers, principals and supervisors, service custodial, and lunchroom personnel [who] also play important roles" (Boykin, 1957, p. 119). Jackson (1940a) had earlier subscribed to this strategy in his evaluation of accreditation in secondary schools for Negroes in the South. His large-scale evaluation of African American secondary schools in the South included a survey of 63 African American high schools in Alabama (sample of 100), a survey of 275 teacher preparation students, and an analysis of the 1930 U.S. Census Reports. But he *also* interviewed 150 college teachers, high school administrators, teachers, professionals, skilled laborers, and semiskilled laborers (both black and white). One wonders what a budget for such an undertaking would look like today!

Jackson's extensive interviews well reflect responsive evaluation's call to seriously consider and address audience requirements for information and to find out what was of value to the specific audience. The views of southern African Americans and Caucasian Americans—teachers, administrators, and laborers alike—were important to consider in any meaningful evaluation of segregated secondary schools. His inclusion of biracial interviews across socioeconomic status was surely a novel approach for his time, particularly since his evaluation focused on *segregated* secondary schools for African Americans. Jackson was another African American visionary who saw the importance of gathering multiple perspectives from stakeholders to produce evaluative findings about the educational opportunities of Negro adolescents in the State of Alabama.

Conclusions

It is clear that African American educational evaluators have been around for a long time. The sample of early African American evaluators presented in this chapter reveals that their work incorporated a number of the major premises articulated in responsive evaluation, notably, the vital importance of qualitative data, of shared lived experiences, and of responsiveness to critical concerns and issues of the members of the setting being evaluated. It appears that their work anticipated significant portions of the literature on responsive evaluation as well as my own work on the inclusion of a culturally relevant perspective in conducting educational evaluations.

There are no simple answers to questions about why the work of these "leaders" has gone unnoticed, or similarly, why people of color do not sit in the seats of power in educational evaluation today. Clearly, early African American educational evaluators did the studies and published in the so-called right journals. But the bulk of their work appeared in the distinguished *Journal of Negro Education,* which was and remains largely unread by the white scholarly community (or at least is not cited in their publications). Some of these African American evaluators worked in close proximity to major figures such as Tyler, Cronbach, Bloom, and others who shaped evaluative thinking on education—but they never made it into the academic inner sanctum. Some may well have been too forceful in their interpretations of evaluative findings. The reasons for their absence in our literature are myriad—but African American evaluators *were* there.

This brief historical analysis is an outgrowth of the Arizona State University Study on Culturally Responsive Evaluation: An African American Perspective, now in its third year. The citations represent but a beginning of the considerable work that remains to be done. Is it time to add the names of Leander Boykin, Reid E. Jackson, Aaron Brown, and others to the pantheon of American educational evaluators for their heretofore unrecognized work? Of course, but it will not do merely to add the names of African American educational evaluators to a reference list here, a bibliography there. We must additionally and aggressively cultivate the rich potential of young scholars of color that lies fallow in the field of educational evaluation as well as others who await admission to our programs of higher education.

Such an effort to welcome more evaluators of color would generate more *efficient and effective* responsive evaluations. Evaluators of color, when evaluating educational programs in settings where our particular cultural groups are intended to be the primary beneficiaries, bring different experiences to the evaluation than do our white evaluator counterparts. Establishing the necessary rapport with principals, teachers, and students in these settings is likely to take us less time because of the probability that a "shared lived experience" exists. Less time will be required in translating the cultural nuances and nonverbal communications associated with observations, conducting interviews, and interpretations that go beyond quantitative indicators of what the program appears to be. Moreover, if we can agree that the responsive evaluator should provide the audience of the report with a "vicarious experience" of what the program is truly like, can we agree that many evaluators have only had a vicarious experience themselves in working with culturally diverse groups? The absence of "direct experiences" or a shared lived experience must surely limit the ability of the evaluator to articulate a vicarious experience of a program nested in a culturally diverse milieu. This is not to suggest that there aren't white educational evaluators who have had a "shared lived" experience in culturally diverse settings. Rather it is to suggest that they are far too few in number, as are evaluators of color.

Well beyond efficiency and effectiveness, the evaluation community has a moral obligation to embrace many more evaluators of color. Early African American evaluators exemplified moral leadership and courage when they used their work to engage the profound political chasms of racism in the mid-twentieth-century United States. Our future as an evaluation community and the importance of our work for our stakeholders depends on our ability to embody similar courage and commitment.

References

American Evaluation Association. "Proposal for The Initiative for Building Diversity Among the Evaluation Community, Phase 1." Submitted to the Kellogg Foundation, Mar. 2000.

American Evaluation Association, Diversity Committee. "American Evaluation Association Statement," Revised, Feb. 1998.

Anderson, J. D. "Toward a History and Bibliography of the Afro-American Doctorate and Professoriate in Education, 1896 to 1980." In A. Bagley (ed.), *The Black Education Professoriate*. SPE Monograph Series. Minneapolis: Society of Professors of Education, 1984.

Anderson, J. D. *The Education of Blacks in the South, 1860–1935*. Chapel Hill: University of North Carolina Press, 1988.

Boykin, L. L. "The Status and Trends in Differentials Between White and Negro Teachers' Salaries in the Southern States 1900–1946." *Journal of Negro Education*, 1949, *18*(4), 40–47.

Boykin, L. L. "Differentials in Negro Education." *Journal of Educational Research*, 1950, *43*(7), 533–540.

Boykin, L. L. "Let's Eliminate the Confusion: What Is Evaluation?" *Educational Administration and Supervision*, 1957, *43*(2), 115–121.

Boykin, L. L. "Negro Publicly Supported Institutions in Louisiana." *Journal of Negro Education*, 1962, *31*(3), 330–340.

Boykin, L. L. "Some Fallacies in the Evaluation and Interpretation of Data Involving the Education of Negroes in the Southern States." *Negro Educational Review*, 1954, *5*(2), 52–58.

Brown v. Board of Education of Topeka, Kansas, 347 U.S. 483, 1954.

Brown, A. "An Evaluation of the Accredited Secondary Schools for Negroes in the South." *Journal of Negro Education*, 1944, *13*(4), 488–498.

Brown, A. "The Education of Negroes in Georgia." *Journal of Negro Education*, 1947, *16*(3), 347–353.

Browne, R. "A Critical Evaluation of Experimental Studies of Remedial Reading and the Report of an Experiment with Groups of Backward Readers." Unpublished doctoral dissertation, Harvard University, 1939.

Chevalier, Z. W., Roark-Calnek, S., and Strahan, D. B. "Responsive Evaluation of an Indian Heritage Studies Program: Analyzing Boundary Definition in a Suburban School Context." Paper presented at the annual meeting of the American Educational Research Association, New York City, Mar. 22, 1982.

Dubois, W.E.B. "Education and Work." *Journal of Negro Education*, 1932, *1*(1), 60–74.

Dubois, W.E.B. "Does the Negro Need Separate Schools?" *Journal of Negro Education*, 1935, *4*(3), 328–335.

Fetterman, D. M. "Empowerment Evaluation." *Evaluation Practice*, 1994, *15*(1), 1–15.

Greene, H. W. *Holders of Doctorates Among American Negroes*. Boston: Meador, 1946.

Greene, J. C. "Evaluation as Advocacy." *Evaluation Practice*, 1997, *18*(1), 25–35.

Greene, M. "The Passions of Pluralism: Multiculturalism and the Expanding Community." *Educational Researcher*, 1993, *22*(1), 13–18.

Hood, S. "Responsive Evaluation Amistad Style: Perspectives of One African American Evaluator." In R. Davis (ed.), *Proceedings of the Stake Symposium on Educational Evaluation*. Urbana-Champaign: University of Illinois, 1998.

Hood, S., and Parker, L. "Minority Bias Review Panels and Teacher Testing for Initial Certification: A Comparison of Two States' Efforts." *Journal of Negro Education*, 1989, *54*(4), 511–520.

Hopson, R. K. "Minority Issues in Evaluation Revisited: Re-conceptualizing and Creating Opportunities for Institutional Change." *American Journal of Evaluation*, 1999, *20*(3), 445–451.

House, E. R. "Evaluation and People of Color: A Response to Professor Stanfield." *American Journal of Evaluation*, 1999, *20*(3), 433–435.

Jackson, R. E. "A Critical Analysis for Educating Secondary School Teachers in Negro Colleges in Alabama." Unpublished doctoral dissertation, The Ohio State University, 1938.

Jackson, R. E. "An Evaluation of Educational Opportunities for the Negro Adolescent in Alabama I." *Journal of Negro Education*, 1940a, *13*(4), 59–72.

Jackson, R. E. "An Evaluation of Educational Opportunities for the Negro Adolescent in Alabama II." *Journal of Negro Education*, 1940b, *13*(4), 200–207.

Madison, A. M. "Introduction." In A. M. Madison (ed.), *Minority Issues in Evaluation*. New Directions in Program Evaluation, no. 53. San Francisco: Jossey-Bass, 1992.

Oak, V. V. "Evaluation of Business Curricula in Negro Colleges." *Journal of Negro Education*, 1938, *7*(1), 19–31.

O'Shea, J. "A Journey to the Midway: Ralph Winfred Tyler." *Educational Evaluation and Policy Analysis*, 1985, *7*(4), 447–459.

Patton, M. Q. "Developmental Evaluation." *Evaluation Practice*, 1994, *15*(3), 311–320.

Patton, M. Q. "Some Framing Questions About Racism and Evaluation: Thoughts Stimulated by Professor John Stanfield's 'Slipping Through the Front Door.'" *American Journal of Evaluation*, 1999, *20*(3), 437–443.

Stake, R. E. "The Countenance of Educational Evaluation." *Teachers College Record*, 1967, *68*(7), 523–540.

Stake, R. E. "Program Evaluation, Particularly Responsive Evaluation." Keynote address at the conference "New Trends in Evaluation," Institute of Education, University of Göteborg, Sweden, Oct., 1973. In G. F. Madaus, M. S. Scriven, and D. L. Stufflebeam (eds.), *Evaluation Models: Viewpoints on Educational and Human Services Evaluation*. Boston: Kluwer-Nijhoff, 1987.

Stanfield, J. H., II. "Slipping Through the Front Door: Relevant Social Scientific Evaluation in the People of Color Century." *American Journal of Evaluation*, 1999, *20*(3), 415–431.

Thompson, C. "Editorial Note: The Availability of Education in the Negro Separate School." *Journal of Negro Education*, 1947, *16*(3), 263–268.

Thompson, C. "Editorial Comment: The Desegregation Decision—One Year Afterward." *Journal of Negro Education*, 1955, *24*(3), 161–164.

Washington, E. L. "An Evaluation of the New York City Junior High School Physical Fitness Tests." Unpublished doctoral dissertation (Ed. D.), New York University, 1935.

Wilcox, T. "Evaluating Programs for Native Students: A Responsive Strategy." Paper presented at the Mokakit Indian Education Research Association's International Conference. London, Ontario, Canada, July 25–27, 1984.

STAFFORD HOOD is associate professor of counseling and counseling psychology in the Division of Psychology in Education at Arizona State University, Tempe. He was recently selected as an American Council on Education Fellow.

4

The profound commitments of a participatory action researcher to engagement with practice and to collaborative inquiry with service providers and service users are historically traced and reflectively analyzed.

Becoming Responsive—and Some Consequences for Evaluation as Dialogue Across Distance

Yoland Wadsworth

> **responsive** *a.* Answering, by way of answer; . . . using responses; responding readily to or *to* some influence, impressionable, sympathetic. . . [**re-** 1. In return, mutual(ly) . . .] [f. L *re(spondere spons-* pledge) . . . **-ive** *suf.* forming *adjs.* w. sense "tending to, having the nature of" . . .

In the mid-1970s under the protective guise of doctoral studies, I limped back into academe for help to understand a couple of life-shaping research and evaluation projects. I was carrying some incomprehensible wounds from the paradigm wars that were then (and are still) being waged in the world of human service practice. In the academy, to my relief, I encountered the "paradigm shift" literature in research (including such scholars as Brian Fay, 1975; Anthony Giddens, 1976; Alvin Gouldner, 1971, 1976; Thomas Kuhn, 1973; Shulamit Reinharz, 1979; Alfred Schutz, 1976; and others) and later its analogue in evaluation in Bob Stake's responsive evaluation (1975) and Michael Patton's (1978, 1980), Peter Reason and John Rowan's (1981) and Egon Guba and Yvonna Lincoln's (1989) takes on utilization-focused, qualitative, collaborative, and constructivist evaluation. This literature supplied a meaningful epistemology for a related methodological move—from reliance on distanced methods of questionnaires and computerized surveys to the use of more powerful critical, interpretivist, ethnographic, grounded, and collaborative approaches.

My inquiry work has been in human services, specifically in early childhood, community health, welfare, and community development. In a way, I think my coming to the new paradigm through human services (rather than Stake's education field), meant I developed a particular take on what responsiveness meant to me in my evaluation work. First, human services rest on a preponderance of more or less highly interventionist professional practices in the lives of mostly adults. To try and conduct evaluative research that does something so apparently simple as to arrange to hear from all the various parties involved is to recast subtle relations of conflicting perspectives, power, and powerlessness that have been built carefully, possibly over decades (Wadsworth, 1997c). This may be, in part, why I appear to have reached somewhat different conclusions from Bob Stake's about the need for empowerment, which is for me not just a nice democratic idea. Rather, I found neither I nor my employing organizations could accomplish evaluation without hearing from service providers *and* end users (clients, patients, students, residents), particularly under conditions that enabled them to speak as they wanted and needed to. In 1975 Bob Stake's audiences that required information may have been more confined to teaching services, educational program practitioners, policymakers, or those requesting evaluation (in contrast to academics). I, too, began by focusing on giving these professional practitioner audiences an effective hearing. However, as I proceeded, the need to include end users became increasingly compelling and simultaneously bewilderingly difficult.

And second, I found the tasks of new service development in human services—to come to agreement on what was of value and why, and how they knew it to be so—never really ended as constant change continuously swept through, year after year.

Three Unfolding Moments

My first moment of becoming a more responsive evaluator essentially involved a substantial broadening of my methodological repertoire. I experienced a methodological epiphany regarding a more responsive "how" of evaluation. My reflections on this transformation are captured in the story of how a nice SPSS user like me came to be a participatory action evaluator. I could see that overly reductionist and one-way methods (Wadsworth, 1982, pp. 233–236) (which I have likened to "reading Braille through a doona"[1]) were a nonresponsive research trap ("I ask, you answer") that cut me off from deeper understanding ("we explore").

The risk or trap of responsiveness was thought to be "to go native." However, as understanding value, merit, worth, or significance was the point of the exercise, it seemed to me logically better to go for properly immersed engagement rather than miss out on "getting it right" in the first place. Once engaged, one could invoke the twin devices of reflective distancing and theorizing driven by the critical values and experiences at hand to help guard against getting overly involved or committed.

Like Bob Stake I think the need for responsiveness calls forth the need for a wide range of methods—such as simple and visual measurement scal-

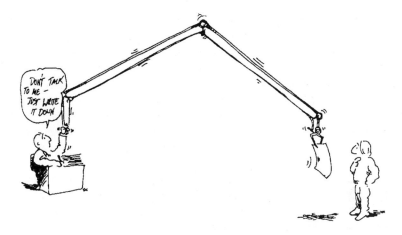

Source: Copyright extract with kind permission from Wadsworth (1997a), p. 45.

ing, ranking, and discrepancy-identifying methods; brainstorming, Delphi, nominal group, and search conference techniques; Open Space Technology, fishbowls, forcefield analysis, concept mapping, critical path and Gantt charts; various voting systems, quality circles, and scenarios, as well as the gamut of pencil and paper, observe-and-discuss, and individual and group interview, conversational, case study, narrative, and storytelling methods. But additionally, as many people's experiences, understandings, and evaluative feedback are more deeply embedded in not-conscious meanings, other methods may be needed to bring out the tacit, to surface the undiscussables, the repressed and suppressed, or to illuminate deeper values or structures operating (for example, memory work, visualization, photography).

My second transformative moment involved the responsive inclusion of more and more groupings of live players or parties who could contribute to the evaluative inquiry. The written proposal for this special volume on responsive evaluation contrasted Bob's reframing of evaluation from a technical effort for distant decision makers to instead comprise "an engagement with onsite practitioners about the quality and meanings of their practice." From practicing in this way I came to the conclusion that it was not only the nominal evaluator who was evaluating, we mostly all were (and are), including the professionals, managers, and policymakers, *and* the service users and local community members. Thus in ordinary daily life, most of us are more or less all the time problematizing or comparing existing situations, practices, or states against possible ones, and deciding what counts as of value and what doesn't, and why. When done well, this accrues as valuable practice wisdom, much like Argyris and Schön's reflective practitioner's tacit knowledge (1974). I found that much of what my evaluative work entailed was unpacking this, only to find that various stakeholders' perceptions rested on untested assumptions about other stakeholders' perceptions.

Gradually I began to try and link the groups and players in increasingly direct exchanges of "data," "findings" and "analysis"—or experience and reflection—*within* the evaluation process. In this process I was also transferring the locus of control from me to more of a "we," and in particular to the bearers of the critical values. I have characterized this as how I progressed from being "messenger" to "go-between" to evaluation "dinner party convenor" (Wadsworth, 1998). As with Bob Stake's claim, I remained a (hopefully) competent and thoughtful researcher and evaluator—but in contrast, I had come to realize that so also, more or less, were they.

Third came the consequences of including ever-widening circles of participants in my evaluation work. As I and my co-evaluators followed the threads of connection among participants out further and further, we came to appreciate and value these connections in their broader, fuller social, emotional, political, and economic contexts. This brought me to the area of systemic thinking, or how people's contexts came to be everything. I also came to believe that evaluators themselves needed to become part of the connections or relationships in a context to be meaningfully responsive. This understanding is elaborated in the next section.

By the end of the 1980s I articulated what seemed to me to be the more responsive and less responsive moments of evaluation in terms of the difference between "open inquiry" and "audit review" (see Table 4.1). And, while the audit review phase can be largely a ticking-off exercise, it nevertheless responds to the needs of players for crucial and clarifying feedback about their activity and achievements. It also requires responsiveness at the "front end" in collaborating with the various players to assemble the questions that will test for the presence, absence or extent of doing what has previously been identified as of merit, worth, value or significance, and at the "back end" in incorporating open inquiry questions to capture what was done that was not to meet the goals and objectives but might nevertheless have been of value (or not).

Evaluation as Dialogue Across Difference and Distance

I had already learned that to omit any relevant party was to store up the possibility of getting it wrong. Additionally, I was learning that the further apart the differing parties' views (the more distinct the discourses), the more the chances for misunderstanding, and the more they needed to be brought into encounter *as part of the evaluation,* and not left unheard and excluded, to fester or react after the submission of any evaluation report. Bob Stake might conceptualize an independent external evaluator, but in practice I found I needed to become part of the participating web of relations to understand the setting and situation.

Table 4.1. Two Approaches to Evaluation.

Open or Inquiry Evaluation	*Audit Review Evaluation*
Inquiry—'to seek'	Audit—'to check'
Starts with the questions: *How are we going? How is this service or activity, etc. going? Is it working? In what ways? What do we think of this service? What is its value?*	Starts with the questions: *Have we done what we set out to do? Is this service, activity, etc. meeting its objectives?*
Asks the comparative questions: *What are we doing?* and *Is that good or bad?* (*What's working? What's not working?*) *What are the signs of this?*	Asks the comparative questions: *What did we set out to achieve?* and *What are the signs we have done this?*
Then asks problem-posing and problem-solving questions: *How could we improve things? How could we do more of what we are doing right? How can we let go of the things we don't want to be doing?*	Then asks the gap-filling and 'irrelevance' eliminating questions: *What are we not doing (that we intended to do)? What are we doing that we shouldn't be (that we didn't intend to)?*
Implies asking: What are the needs?	Implies already assuming what are the needs.
The questions are 'opening up' questions implying the need to build theory from diverse sources. (There isn't necessarily a concrete picture of what the answer would look like at the outset.) The process will involve repeatedly asking the question *Why are we doing this?* until the fullest and most satisfying set of explanations is achieved.	The questions are 'narrowing down' questions, implying the need to test theory from pre-existing sources. (The correct answers are already known and are merely being checked for their existence and implementation.) The process will involve repeatedly asking the questions, *Are we doing this?, Are we doing that?* until the full set of possible aimed-for activities have been checked for.
Starts with immediate or obvious 'problematisation' (either of good features or of bad features)—leaves non-problematic as taken for granted.	Sets out systematically to problematise all possible activities—leaves 'nothing' as taken for granted (except matters not covered by goals, objectives and aims).
Examines practice in order to be able to extract assumptions and intentions. Can then develop new and improved evaluative criteria:	Examines practice in the light of objectives (applies known evaluative criteria):
Thus can ask about possible new goals, objectives, aims and activities that might differ from current ones. Is developmental (or feedback or 'cybernetic' systemic). Is improvement and change-oriented.	Thus starts and ends with existing goals, objectives, aims and activities. Is closed and linear systemic. Is status-quo (or frozen snapshot) oriented.
Requires a questioning, intuitive, observant (interpretive), inquisitive, imaginative, speculative and creative mind. Use of logic of discovery. Feels more like an art. Aiming at excellence of achievement. Looks for 'meaningfuls'.	Requires a systematic, orderly, observant (monitoring), fastidious, highly organised, analytical mind. Use of logic of accounting. Feels more like a craft. Aiming at competence of performance. Looks for 'measurables'.
Relies on who is/are the inquirer/s.	Relies on the quality of previously agreed-upon goals, objectives and aims (and level of consensus previously reached).

Source: Copyright extract with kind permission from Wadsworth (1997b), p. 45, Diagram 3.

Separate Parties to Evaluation

Source: Reproduced with permission from the online journal *Action Research International,* 1998, paper 2, p. 8.

In 1984 I identified four conceptual parties or reference groups (see 1997a, pp. 17–18) and explicated these further (see 1997b, pp. 12–18) as a way of answering the question "for who or for what, is the evaluand?":

- The evaluator or evaluators
- The evaluated
- Those for whom the evaluation is primarily intended (the group the evaluand is ultimately to help, meet their needs, address their interests, solve their problem, and so forth)
- Those for whom evaluation is also intended (in the secondary sense of informing, guiding, inspiring, influencing or convincing regarding how to act best for the group primarily to benefit from the evaluand; to assist them in their work with or as part of the evaluand, making policy for it, or funding of it, and so forth)

Identifying who composes the third of these four groups has been my way of working to more or less agreement about the compass direction or perspective around which the different parties to the evaluation come together (Wadsworth, 1997b, pp. 12–18). Chief among strategies for retaining the guiding perspective of the primary beneficiary or reference group (what I have called the *critical reference group*) throughout the evaluation, has been to ensure that members of the critical reference group are actively present in, driving, and anchoring the core of the inquiry group itself.

In transforming my own position away from central driver and receiver and repository of data provided by the various parties, I was now aiding a process of the various parties (including myself) getting access to *each others'* experiences, insights, and differing perspectives and receiving any collectively generated new data, information, or input (Wadsworth, 2000). To achieve this, I (and we) have experimented with ways for the group to self-inform (such as Do It Yourself group interviewing, strategic questionnaires, round robins, or on-the-spot question sheets that are then stuck up around the walls for people to read and discuss) as well as to be able to more truly hear each other. I will also provide resources for groups in whatever ways possible, such as through the supply of material from published literature and other visual aids to thinking.

The extension of evaluation to take into account ever-broader cultural, organizational, physical, social, political, and economic environment contexts, as well as ever-widening circles of stakeholders, whether "in flight" formative or "after the event" summative, has meant for my own work that the bigger the evaluand, the bigger the octopus of an evaluation project—with multiplying tentacles! In a large systems project focusing on consumer evaluation of acute psychiatric hospital practice, we commenced from any single patient's experience in a single ward, and worked out and up with all the varying stakeholders, through the entire state mental health services system to eventually connect with federal policymaking.

I now think the endless back and forth, and connecting up of groups in dialogue, is a bit like knitting socks on twenty-four needles. This in turn for me—although maybe not for Bob Stake—shifts the role of the nominal evaluator to one of more or less responsive orchestrator and emergent design facilitator.

But nor is this mere group work or group facilitation; it is profoundly evaluative activity. In the course of deeply engaged evaluation practice, responsive co-evaluators will work with the comparative framework of evaluative thinking and co-construct recognizable theory of more or less great power (see, for

Collaborating Parties to Evaluation

Source: Reproduced with permission from the online journal *Action Research International,* 1998, paper 2, p. 12.

example, Wadsworth and Epstein, 1996, pp. 148–175). I have found, diverging from Bob Stake's idea that generalizable theory is not possible, that frequently this grounded theory will be in similar territory to (but not the same as) the thinking of some recognized academic theorists. It has, however, to meet a harder test than those theoreticians. Improved practice evaluation theory or logic can't just seem plausible in a journal article. It has to work in practice. Here then is the value of praxis—relying on phronesis: the well-theorized and wisely lived orbits of people in collective social, emotional, political, and economic life. (See the chapter by Thomas Schwandt in this volume for further discussion of the connections of responsive evaluation to praxis and phronesis.) This is not predictive theory. It is however possibilistic theory—offered in dialogue across differing contexts and sites, and able to be taken up, tested, and modified elsewhere.

Lewin's action research maxim that the best way to try and understand an organization is to change it has seemed to me to mean naturalistic, evaluative co-inquirers are acting as change agents as they move through both small and large cycles of reflecting, observing, discussing, theorizing, concluding, planning, acting, reflecting, observing, and so on.

The following example of commencing an evaluative inquiry effort serves to introduce the final discussion regarding the need for deeper dialogue to bridge gaps and to engender understandings about what counts as of merit, value, worth, and significance in the eyes of all relevant stakeholders, and particularly through the lens of the critical stakeholder.

Getting (and Not Getting) to Responsive Evaluative Dialogue

The Aboriginal Liaison Officer from the capital city office of a state government department rang me to see if I could help a local rural-regional center "get up" a community recreation plan. It involved determining what would be of most value, so as to set the right goals and then be able to work toward the best form of successful implementation.

Competent-looking plans had been written by contract consultants in other regions, but for this region he thought it might be good to see if we could "get the local people involved." He didn't want elaborate expert surveying, just "some yarns" really. That way the plan might not stay high and dry after a consultant moved on, and maybe it could better get at what the people really needed. He'd heard I did that sort of thing.

At the first meeting at the Koorie Community Centre, after some polite preliminaries, we moved to the meeting room where a semicircle of lounge chairs was occupied by a small handful of the local Koorie people, mostly women. Others hovered in the background, watching. Facing the lounge chairs was a straighter line of hard-back meeting chairs in which "we" sat: state and regional government officers and I. Apart from the Liaison Officer we were all "gubs" (from *Gubba*—Aboriginal word for non-Aboriginal European-ancestry people, originating in the English word *government*).

I asked the local Koorie people about "the things going on about sport and recreation." I heard the answers as quiet, polite, tentative, unengaged. I fished deeper: "sport and rec," I said, "could be anything they might be doing." Silence. Pushing it to the limits of a discourse that would still connect with the well-suited folk sitting with their papers and briefcases alongside my right-hand field of vision, I asked an open question, "What's going on here at the moment; what is, perhaps, concerning you?" One of the women stirred, hesitated, then leaned forward slightly and addressed the carpet in a quiet voice, "well we are worried about our young people. . . ."—the departmental officers turned their gaze toward her—"the ones that were taken away."[2]

The government officers looked away again. Not relevant. Welfare issue. Another department's business.

I followed the spark of interest. "What have you been thinking about that one?" "Well. . . ." [eyes still firmly down] "Trouble with the police. And joy-rides and that. We'd like to take them on a camp." At the word *camp* the sport and recreation folks' attention was engaged again. She continued, "We'd like to talk to them, about our ways, Koorie ways, and make them proud again so they know who they are."

"A camp," said the smartly dressed young sport and recreation woman officer brightly, "we have a camp you could use for that." She named an under-cover camp, which I assumed to be nearby in the region somewhere. I looked back at the Koorie women's faces but they showed no signs of even acknowledging the offer. Nor did the Koorie men's. The Aboriginal Liaison Officer wasn't saying anything, either. Hmm. Silence descended. Navigating by embodied emotion, searching for the right response, I mentally computed various questions, with each possibly leading to an endgame. A mental file labeled "experience of Aboriginal communities" yielded a faint memory and I thought to respond, "Have you got a camp of your own?" "Yes," they said, naming their camping place. Bingo!

It seemed this did not appear to the departmental officers to be as cheap and handy a camp as that suggested by them, and the meeting came to an end with a crisply stated request for a detailed written and costed proposal.

But they did find a procedure that might admit the people's own camp proposal. Nevertheless, it was clear it would need plenty of informal, off-stage caucusing and consultation, message-carrying, and small yarns, as well as just being around the community center to build anything like the communication relations needed. As we drove back toward the metropolis, the government Aboriginal Liaison Officer and the local Koorie elder sat chortling with that discrete tinge of bitterness that is never quite offensive, but alerts to something else going on.

I inquired.

He said, "You know that camp the sport and rec folk suggested? Well, that used to be a home the [Aboriginal] children were taken away to."

Conflict and Evaluation as Dialogue Across Difference and Distance

Many of us are now experimenting with processes that both allow the least powerful voices to express themselves as they want and need to, and safeguard the morale and affirm the good values held by the more powerful as they try to hear. And we struggle also with the far more challenging reverse task. In the cartoon of all the parties to an evaluation coming to the table, a rather heart-warming scene is depicted of distances eliminated and mutual respect and understanding unfolding.

It is rarely so easy or quick—or necessarily even possible. Sometimes all parties literally can't bear to hear each other. Sometimes the dialogic partners may never actually come to the table to meet face to face, and sometimes they might meet only at the end. Pluralism does not go uncontested—even unwittingly by those who might most believe in its value. Human services professionals, very committed to serving, to caring and to meeting others' needs, may also unwittingly disempower, use hurtful or stigmatizing language, routinely second-guess the needs of their clients, patients, and consumers, and impose solutions without asking or checking. They may also be surprised, hurt, and wounded when there is a negative reaction. And it is often not a benign issue of expert wisdom having forgotten the consumer's perspective, needing only its inclusion. It may be a matter of the consumer's experience being systematically not sought. In turn, service providers may feel silenced or their knowledge and expertise discounted. In the background, silent, is the matter of one party earning money from the encounter, often very good money, and the other party not, and maybe being quite impoverished.

Conflict and apparently incommensurable discourses may be routine.

To give a single example (from the acute psychiatry consumer evaluation work) of profoundly differing evaluative discourses:

> What may have been experienced by some consumers as "abuse, humiliation or neglect, emotional blackmail and atrocity" may instead for some staff have been "limit-setting, standard treatment, individual service-planning and an incident." What might be for some staff "safe seclusion, necessary medication, a successful treatment option in x% of cases, unavoidable duty of care and behavioural modification" can be for many consumers "being locked up, forcibly injected, electrically shocked till you lost your memory, being assaulted, and treated like an animal." What can be for some consumers "frightening powerlessness and terror," can be for some staff "therapeutic restraint and temporary ideation" [Wadsworth and Epstein, 1998, p. 374].

Under these conditions we have, like others, developed a range of techniques for deeper exchange. These include the use of the formal technique of dialogue, employing special techniques to avoid discussion, debate or argumentation; using linguistic forms such as "that makes me think about . . " or "what

I'm thinking now is . . "; being neither adversarial nor consensus- or decision-oriented; "sitting with" conflict, even in silence; having people speak for themselves ("I") and not on behalf of others ("they" or "we"); promoting focused listening and the giving of attention to others' and to one's own reactions.

But it remains remarkably difficult to build in. Instead there continues to be regular resort to numerous quickie audit-style evaluations, or to expert top-down and nonparticipatory approaches. It seems so much more efficient to reach for certainty and control—over the evaluator, the evaluated, the time, the outcomes, and all the other specifications at the outset. And it seems more efficient to leave out those who are on the receiving end of human services, or to keep their input tightly constricted by prechosen, closed questions on mailed questionnaires.

Thus there is a new range of puzzles associated with the new paradigm of "responsive connectedness" or of "naturalistic inquiry" or "critical constructivism." How to ensure, for example, that people (particularly the critical reference group) raise their evaluative questions explicitly rather than allow situations to remain taken-for-granted, unproblematized, or buried under pressure of being undiscussable? How to ensure that all the relevant parties come together and stay together—including the most powerful and the least powerful—and that one of these does not leave if the other is seen as having too great a voice? How to take the time for the maximum possible listening, observing, and talking, in sufficient detail and allowing sufficient reflection time to enable real breakthroughs? How to minimize the centralization of data (especially if the methods are not in themselves very democratic) and instead find ways of sharing the raw data so analyses can be more collective? Even in the small, local, and specific, how can participants press for deeper underlying explanations that will provide some bigger maps for at least an immediate future? How to build into a nominal fieldwork phase, alongside interviews and observations, space for asking participants what they think should be the desirable criteria for judging the evaluand, thus avoiding exclusion of their views from program judgments? How to ensure there is sufficient time as part of the process for going back to people: checking meanings, checking the extent of real consensus against the appearance of such, and checking that the apparent next steps are really seen as the best next steps? And finally, how to build into the design the *full* cycle of open inquiry and audit review steps including implementation, monitoring, further refinement, new needs assessment, and the generation and monitoring of new purposes?

I have been involved with this kind of dialogue work—or what my friend and colleague Jacques Boulet has termed *multilogue*—across difference and distance in a number of different settings (Wadsworth, 1998). And I see my own evaluative activity situating itself increasingly in the middle of various bifurcations, or multifurcations, not as catalyst or unchanged cipher for change, but necessarily changing responsively also. Each time I am involved thus, I am struck both by how necessary and at the same time how very difficult it is. It seems to be similar to the task of any who are trying to build bridges between different perspectives or warring camps, whether they are marital partners, racial or ethnic groups, citizenry and government, or business and environment advocates. They seem to be the tasks of reknitting community, of reconnecting isolated folk who have local knowledge into connected collectivities of people who together can become mutually knowledgeable and effectively make the necessary judgments. Whether trying to create safe communities, caring human services, efficient organizations, coherent cultures, healthier food, better built environments, educated populations, or sustainable economies, at the bottom of any dispute are differing perceptions, differing interests, and differing formulations of what is of value, merit, worth, or significance. And at the bottom of any evaluation is an attempt to adjudicate these.

Not everyone will want to be involved in this kind of work. But those of us who are prepared to put on these new wings of possibility will look to our colleagues to support us in what we do, just as they need us to recognize their place in the scheme of things that results from a new consensus.

Concluding Words

I don't think of what I do as responsive evaluation as a kind of exotic variant. I think what I do is standard mainstream evaluation *in its context*. And that context is one

- of complexity, uncertainty, change and paradox,
- in which it is thought that all parties have formed valuable ways of understanding merit, worth, value, and significance that would be useful if known, and
- where one of those parties is recognized as the intended primary beneficiary of the evaluand and is believed to have literally critical things to say about it if it is to be accurately resonant with their needs as experienced by them.

Though the conditions listed here are distinctive, they are not at all uncommon. Human services and their programs, funding, and policies are always in a state (or context) of more or less change because the situations of providers, users, communities, and global societies are also always changing. Differing stakeholders always see differently and these differences may become difficulties and conflicts if there are threats and fears—particularly along the staff-consumer bifurcation and given that service users mostly have less power than service providers. There is also a growing realization that human services exclude their service users from evaluative and planning decision making at their own very great risk—whether risk of adverse incidents or of not meeting people's needs.

Under all these conditions I daily see around me evidence that mainstream service evaluations are taking on more and more of the characteristics of what I think of as the responsiveness that I and others have long proposed as essential to the task of evaluation. For example:

- The use of more two-way methods, including group discussions and face-to-face engagement
- The use of multiple methods to pick up different views and differing kinds of views (including increasing use of peer-led questioning)
- The explicit inclusion of multiple stakeholders' differing views in the conduct of the evaluation, including on evaluation project committees or as co-evaluators
- The inclusion or extension of pilot or preliminary work, and postreview follow-up or work, as well as talk of dialogue and emergent or iterative elements (such as under the rubric of organizational development, the learning organization, or continuous improvement) to extend the evaluation's iterativity and longitudinality

Yet one of the hardest challenges of all remains the active inclusion of the critical reference group—primarily service users—even when this might be stipulated in the tender brief. The phenomenon of how to surface critical discrepancies that may have been carefully suppressed or repressed—when not surfacing them means continued tolerance of poor quality or even damaging services, but surfacing them means pain and defensive reactions—has become a focus of my current thinking. At present my best take on this is the analogue of deep tissue remedial massage. The skilled massage therapist starts gently, easing deeper as the muscles relax, trusting the inquisitive careful probing that finds its way responsively. The ultimate work is the equivalent to pressure that would have left a bruise if it had been less responsive and more forced. Though slow, gentle, and iterative, this is nevertheless active going forward, and not continued toleration of things as they are. When I have helped achieve this in my evaluative inquiry work I mostly see the "them" and "us" becoming part of a new "we" who, if at all possible, *come to resonance* around the critical party's situation. Thereafter, together, the parties may better identify, implement, and monitor jointly agreed purposes and practices of merit, value, worth, and significance. As Michael Quinn Patton has so nicely put this potentially mutual responsiveness: "Much of what evaluation involves is coming to see the other person's perspective" (1995, personal communication).

The achieving of this kind of communicative competence remains therefore a live goal for those of us working in these kinds of evaluation settings, especially across differences, distances, and apparently incommensurable discourses.

Notes

1. A doona is a feather coverlet or eiderdown.
2. The issue of the children "taken away" later became a national human rights issue. Called "the stolen generation," it was the result of fifty years of church and government welfare practice of taking the children of mixed (European and Aboriginal) parentage, and adopting them out to white couples or placing them in institutions.

References

Argyris, C., and Schön, D. *Theory in Practice: Increasing Professional Effectiveness.* San Francisco: Jossey-Bass, 1974.

Fay, B. *Social Theory and Political Practice.* London: Allen & Unwin, 1975.

Giddens, A. *New Rules of Sociological Method: A Positive Critique of Interpretive Sociologies.* London: Hutchinson, 1976.

Gouldner, A. *The Coming Crisis of Western Sociology.* London: Heinemann, 1971.

Gouldner, A. *The Dialectic of Ideology and Technology: The Origins, Grammar and Future of Ideology.* London: Macmillan, 1976.

Guba, E. G., and Lincoln, Y. S. *Fourth Generation Evaluation.* Thousand Oaks, Calif.: Sage, 1989.

Kuhn, T. *The Structure of Scientific Revolutions.* Chicago: University of Chicago Press, 1973.

Patton, M. Q. *Utilization-Focused Evaluation.* Thousand Oaks, Calif.: Sage, 1978.

Patton, M. Q. *Qualitative Evaluation Methods.* Thousand Oaks, Calif.: Sage, 1980.

Reason, P., and Rowan, J. (eds.) *Human Inquiry: A Sourcebook of New Paradigm Research.* Chichester, England: Wiley, 1981.

Reinharz, S. *On Becoming a Social Scientist: From Survey Research and Participant Observation to Experiential Analysis.* San Francisco: Jossey-Bass, 1979.

Schutz, A. *The Phenomenology of the Social World.* London: Heinemann, 1976.

Stake, R. E. *Evaluating the Arts in Education: A Responsive Approach.* Columbus, Ohio: Merrill, 1975.

Wadsworth, Y. "The Politics of Social Research," *Australian Journal of Social Issues,* 1982, 17(3), 232–246.

Wadsworth, Y. *Do It Yourself Social Research.* Sydney: Allen & Unwin, 1997a.

Wadsworth, Y. *Everyday Evaluation on the Run.* Sydney: Allen & Unwin, 1997b.

Wadsworth, Y. "Partnering a Powerful Paradox: Consumer Evaluation of Psychiatric Hospital Practice." In R. LaBonte (ed.), *Power, Participation and Partnerships for Health Promotion.* Carlton South, Victoria: Victorian Health Promotion Foundation, 1997c.

Wadsworth, Y. "'Coming to the Table': Some Conditions for Achieving Consumer-Focused Evaluation of Human Services by Service-Providers and Service Users." *Evaluation Journal of Australasia,* 1998, 10(1 and 2), 11–29.

Wadsworth, Y. "The Mirror, the Magnifying Glass, the Compass and the Map—Facilitating Participatory Action Research." In P. Reason and H. Bradbury (eds.), *Handbook of Action Research.* London: Sage, 2000.

Wadsworth, Y., and Epstein, M. *Understanding and Involvement (UandI): Consumer Evaluation of Acute Psychiatric Hospital Practice,* Vol. 3: *A Project Concludes.* Melbourne: VM IAC, 1996.

Wadsworth, Y., and Epstein, M. "Building In Dialogue Between Consumers and Staff in Acute Mental Health Services." *Systemic Practice and Action Research,* 1998, 11(4), 353–379.

YOLAND WADSWORTH has worked as a research and evaluation practitioner and facilitator for twenty-nine years. She is a coordinator of the community-based Melbourne Action Research Issues Centre, a senior academic associate in social inquiry and community studies at Victoria University, and adjunct professor in the Institute for Social Research at Swinburne University of Technology.

5

The meanings of responsive evaluation are critiqued and reinterpreted through the lenses of loyalty and betrayal, direction and indirection, openings and closures. The hidden and unspeakable aspects of responsive evaluation are thereby deconstructively revealed.

The Changing Face of Responsive Evaluation: A Postmodern Rejoinder

Ian Stronach

> Finishing a case study is a consummation of a work of art (Stake, 1995, p. 136).

> Art is that practice which in its utter uselessness, constantly escapes, exceeds, all attempts to press it into the service of theory and knowledge (Phillipson, 1989, p. 166).

The purpose of this chapter is to offer a deconstructive rereading of key themes in Bob Stake's work on "responsive evaluation," taking that term to be a broad reference and implication running through his work. The chapter draws on earlier work on "new paradigm" research (Stronach, 1997), which reinterpreted the various inaugurations of Parlett and Hamilton, Reason and Rowan, and Glaser and Strauss (Stronach, 1999a). Stake's work on evaluation and case study, described in those earlier accounts as a "founding reference and paradigm marker" (1997, p. 23), continues to be important because it holds open a set of possibilities for educational meaning (a quasi-descriptive space), in the face of the normative closures of "effectiveness" discourses (Lyotard, 1984). These discourses seek to close down on pluralities and differences not legislated for in global and national measures of student against student, school against school, and system against system: "So, as skepticism grows, as postmodern doubts become more somber, there is, at the same time, an upscaling of rational, measurement-driven, systemic reform, with a greater demand for standardization and all at a more frenzied pace" (Stake, 1997, p. 45).

Much more could be said about such discourses (Power, 1997; Strathern, 2000; Stronach, 1999b; Tsoukas, 1997). Let us note here only that they seem to have created in Stake a note of elegiac gloom, a feeling that *educational* moments in their singularity and uniqueness are draining from the educational system, from the very possibility of educational research's noticing, and that to improve we now have to conserve: "Because it is an exercise in such depth, the study [educational case study] is an opportunity to see what others have not yet seen, to reflect the uniqueness of our own lives, to engage the best of our interpretive powers, *and to make, even by its integrity alone, an advocacy for those things we cherish*" (Stake, 1995, p. 136, emphasis added). Something of the spirit of Canute in there.

Naturally, a language of integrity, depth, and uniqueness is enough to make a postmodernist begin to quiver, but rather than jumping at the labels of modernist discourse, the intention here is to consider what it would mean to *respond well* to Stake's meticulous responsiveness to the case, the self, the audience, the cause of disinterestedness, and the business of education as opposed to schooling. Where among such concerns *should* a deconstructive purchase be made? And for what purpose? According to House and Howe, such a question takes us immediately into self-contradiction: postmodernists see knowledge as "merely a mask for self-interest and power" (House and Howe, 1999, p. 82) and hence a recipe for "moral-political inaction" (p. 74). The "postmodernist attack on reason nullifies *all* knowledge claims" and results in "hyperpluralism" (pp. 85, 86; emphasis in original). While such straw-man polemics are easily countered,[1] it is important to *perform* alternatives, to put prescriptions into action. This deconstruction is intended to reassure even such "deliberative hermeneuticists" that postmodernists are capable of a political reading.

So where should a deconstructive purchase be made?[2] Methodological texts on evaluation are most interesting when they combine theory and practice, when they also show their evolution and growth—to echo the metaphors of responsive evaluation deployed elsewhere in this book. In such a constellation, principles, cases, theories, tips, roles, arguments, developments, and reminiscence jostle in a rich resource for deconstruction. Such a text is Bob Stake's (1995) *The Art of Case Study Research.* The text offers an overview of an evaluation philosophy, and also relates back to earlier work. The aim of this deconstruction is to look at Stake's texts as a series of movements between theory and practice, and then more politically in contrast with House and Howe's recent and influential *Values in Evaluation and Social Research* (1999). Overall, the deconstruction will aim to be "faithful to the text's self-betrayal" (Stronach and MacLure, 1997, p. 141, echoing Kamuf),[3] and to look for that treachery as an "internal necessity" (p. 23). Where, then, can such a search begin?

Best start with *nothing,* and ask how it got there.

Forging the "Space" of Responsiveness

> The possibility of forgery always defines the very structure of the event called signature [Weber, 1995, p. 25].

Elsewhere in this book, *responsiveness* starts with a definition (its signature), and then evolves. It is a discovery, a new object of knowledge and possibility for learning. It develops (re-signs). Spreads. Becomes the occasion of this book itself, folding out from itself in acts of elaboration and proliferation. But here, in this chapter, it is inaugurated as a *nothing,* a lack, one that is invented as such, true only in its effects. Stake's early evaluation model—"countenance"—was prompted by the *absence* of "full description"; it was holism's *lack* before it became an addition (Stake, 1967, pp. 54, 55). In a typical "metaphysics of pure presence" (Derrida, 1977, p. 236), Stake sought to bring into educational view the "full countenance of evaluation" (Stake, 1967, p. 52). It seemed that this fullness (also a completeness, usefulness, naturalness, spontaneity) defined more than anything else what it was to be "responsive":

> A responsive approach to evaluation . . . is comprehensive in nature and takes into account the many critical factors that characterize . . . teaching and learning [Bloom, 1975, p. 3]. . . .
> Great attention is given to the description and judgment needs of those who commission the conduct of an evaluation [Popham, 1975, p. 32]. . . .
> Responsive studies are organised around phenomena encountered—often unexpectedly—as the programme goes along [Stake, 1976, p. 20].

Such an approach would be more useful, because comprehensive. It would translate "formal communication" into "natural communication" (Stake, 1976, p. 14). Like Parlett and Hamilton and Reason and Rowan after him, Stake sought a "naturalistic" opportunity for educational inquiry: "holistic," "vicarious," capturing the "mystery of the experience" (p. 23). In a similar way, "naturalism" was a technology of representation that denied itself as such. Stake's own subscription to such "naturalizations" is vivid in the active verbs with which his case studies "grow," "live," "emerge," and "evolve" (Stake, 1995, pp. 21, 32). The case is an "entity," "in some ways has a unique life" (p. 20). It even has a "self" (p. 2). These metaphors are not innocent and it is unsurprising that he can write of research participants, counter to his constructivist temper, as "the people who *belong to* the case" (p. 20). It is the case that lives, grows, and owns. Stake the case-writer is like a back-to-front television cook: "here's one I didn't make earlier."

But what constructed the nothing out of which Stake constructed the something of responsiveness to fill it? The answer seems to lie, surprisingly, in the couplet "stimulus-response." Stake sought their "reversal": "were he to have had more direct ties with the anthropologist, the journalist, and the poet, the contemporary evaluator might have reversed the S–R arrangement" (Stake, 1975, p. 21). To respond, then, meant to wait, to *not* stimulate, to attend to the "natural ways in which people assimilate information and arrive at understanding" (p. 23): "Qualitative study capitalizes on ordinary ways of making sense" (p. 72).

So the new research, in the eyes of the old at least, was to *do* nothing.[4] Waiting became a form of research action. But it was to do nothing purposefully, in the interests of "natural" ways of attending, learning, and telling. That perspective would upend the dichotomies of preconception, instrumentality, and closure (p. 16).

Such epistemological spaces are twice-filled: once with what makes it possible for them to appear; twice with what makes it possible for them to *re-present*. At first Stake made possible that re-presenting space by opening a gap between "description" and "judgment": "Description is one thing, judgment is another" (Stake, 1967, p. 55). The researcher would describe, the professional educator judge. Thus roles were also separated. At the same time he elevated these ideas and roles as the "two basic acts of evaluation": "To be fully understood, the educational program must be fully described and fully judged" (p. 54).

This "lift and separate" scenario for the "fuller" figure of evaluation—a kind of Wonderbra epistemology—did not last long.[5] As House and Howe have noted, it was hard to hold on to a position that description and judgment were separable, when fact/value dichotomous paradigms were in free fall.[6] Stake had found (founded rather than found), therefore, a nothing and filled it with something that then turned out to be nothing. There was no defensible gap between description and judgment, or not as he had first conceived it. And to this he confessed. But that nothing had a positive consequence that endured nevertheless because the illusory gap between description and judgment had opened up the possibility of a constituency of judges who could be fed descriptions in order to produce their own reasoned judgments of educational events. The play of description and judgment provoked its own audience, even if it came to nothing itself. Out of *double nothing* came something, a real "audience," a point of origin for "stakeholders." In turn, evaluation came to be reconstructed as essentially a social communication rather than a technical representation.[7] Stake had "animated" methodology, brought it to life (and as we will later argue, in so doing threatened to kill it off): "It is interactive communication, first between a single researcher with the case, later with the reader. The exercise is partly commiseration, partly celebration, but always intellectualization, a conveying, a creating of meaning" (Stake, 1995, p. 136).

Note that "commiseration" and "celebration" precede "intellectualization": the priority is the evaluator "living" and being in the space opened up by responsiveness. Without that enlivenment the evaluator cannot think well. Evaluation comes to be an emplotment ("what is happening?" Stake, 1975, p. 15). It is a matter of "chronologies more than causes and effects"

(Stake, 1995, p. 39), provoking individual judgment or community partic-ipation with the other actors in the evaluation scenario:[8] "He [or she] gets program personnel to react to the accuracy of his proposals; authority fig-ures to react to the importance of various findings; and audience members to react to the relevance of his findings (Stake, 1975, p. 14).

In this way, then, theory's *lack* inaugurated the process through which theory (of evaluation as description versus judgment, or fact versus value) could later be displaced and reinvented by practice. The ability of the "audience" to judge cases, and indeed the evaluator's "collected" judgments of the case, could then be asserted on the basis of "naturalistic generaliza-tion." "Naturalistic generalization" cured the fact/value epistemological problem by displacing it from the evaluator to the audience: the problem was exported. As an export, it was a solution rather than a problem. "Nat-uralistic generalizations" had a further benefit: unlike formalistic general-izations, they could not be wrong. Make of it what you will, offered the evaluator: that is both your right and your responsibility in a democratic society. Thus what we might call "description-judgments" could be *socially* rather than epistemologically legitimated, and a "live" audience installed to make them. At the same time, and paradoxically, judgment was priva-tized from the "public sector" of research methodology to the "private sec-tor" of individual judgment: that was the "audience's" responsibility, just as it was the evaluator's to concentrate on the singularities of the case. In this way both evaluator and stakeholder could retreat to their own indi-vidualisms, safe in the belief that each had been granted due right to the truth. "The real business of case study is particularization, not generaliza-tion" (Stake, 1995, p. 8).

Given this move to a more interactive and social mode of inquiry, "responsiveness" became more iterative than sequential, as Stake's respon-sive "clock" had earlier suggested: "On this clock, however, any event can follow any event, many events occur simultaneously, and the evaluator returns to each event many times" (Stake, 1975, p. 18). The clock face of responsive evaluation now ticked to a more erratic and less systemic beat. And naturalism could also offer method to the evaluator, as against the dis-ciplines of "social-science-oriented" (Stake, 1995, p. 39) research. "Natural" methods of listening, understanding, and telling engendered research that in some senses *promised* to go native. Indeed, it offered an anti-discipline of "naturalness," taking the opposite view to the disciplines, which aimed to transcend the "natural" in order to demystify it. Out of a double nothing, then, a double something. Or we might put it this way: that the cast of responsive evaluation moved *somewhat* from a representational to a consen-sual view of truth, from an epistemological to a political justification. The responsive evaluator offered to be present (celebrating, commiserating, learn-ing, educating), to be absent (speaking only the registers of the participants), to be doubly absent in a methodological sense (naturalistic methods and the-ories), and to be additionally absent in terms of not contaminating the case with personal values (a "facilitator," a "civil servant," Stake 1995, p. 33; 1975, p. 36). Once present and three times absent, the evaluator could claim those absences as a *present* (a gift as well as a presence) for the empowerment of the subjects. And because the participants did not need to be fed judgments any longer, they could be re-presented—at least in a certain light—as "franchised member[s] of the transaction" (Stake, 1995, p. 122). "The reader will take both our narrative descriptions and our assertions: narrative descriptions to form vicarious experience and naturalistic generalizations, assertions to work with existing propositional knowledge to modify existing generalizations" (p. 86).

That still left vacant, or at least uncertain, the positive space wherein the evaluator could hope to differentiate between descriptions and judgments, or facts and values. The first tactic was to entext the evaluator as an object for reader inspection: "better to give the reader a good look at the researcher" (Stake, 1995, p. 95). If the writer provided a personal biographical description, the reader might judge the writer and the trustworthiness of the account.[9] The second was to revert to a positivist view of what it was that evaluators collected as data:[10] "providing readers with good raw material for their own generalizing" (p. 102). The reader could judge over the writer's (self-effacing) shoulder. The third was to read the readers' minds for them: "providing information easily assimilated with the readers' existing knowledge" (p. 126). The fourth was to concede the uniqueness of both reader and researcher, accepting the slippages of individuality: "Each researcher contributes uniquely to the study of the case; each reader derives unique meanings" (p. 103). Finally, the researcher had an obligation that readers themselves might fail to appreciate: "to liberate the reader from simplistic views" (p. 99). Fact/value, it seemed, had not so much been abandoned as had fragmented into a series of shards of difference, each of which reflected a varying sort of difference and perspective of one surface upon the other—a hall of mirrors rather than windows. Some of these complemented each other, and were addressed in terms of Stake's consensual notion of "triangulation" (Stake, 1995, p. 107); some contradicted—but all relied in the end on distinctions between fact and value being upheld. From their "collection" Stake offered, as he has said elsewhere in this book, a "softly framed" judgment that could always be read otherwise.

Yet Stake's *Art*, which we might recall made a final appeal to *integrity,* to the resistance of advocacy and promotionalism (responsiveness's temptations), seems to this writer grounded more in an appeal to moral authority than to any epistemological or philosophical appeal: "*to make, even by its integrity alone, an advocacy for those things that we cherish*" (Stake, 1995, p. 136, my emphasis again). One could see in this a pluralistic triangulation, or, more positively from a postmodernist perspective, a healthy abandonment of methodology (that fantasy of universality) as opposed to method. Integrity turns out to be an eclectic thing. We could try to spring a surprise: can Stake be recruited to the postmodern?

The Indirection of Methodology

> One of the features of power (one of its effects) is precisely to escape from a real or logical order [Gil, 1998, p. 4].

The first section of this chapter has been about the (allegedly) serendipitous emergence of a particular methodology and a model for evaluation; the second will try to make them disappear.

The first *nothing,* it will be recalled, was an absence caused by "reductionism" and "elementalism" (Stake, 1995, p. 47)—a disciplinary flaw. It inaugurated a "responsive" space for description that in turn might then recognize, express, and communicate multiplicity and uniqueness. Only such an account could access "the unique complexity of the case" (Stake, 1995, p. 63). To understand the openness of educational events and their essential indeterminacy meant treating "the uniqueness of individual cases" (p. 39). Thus "countenance" came to involve both a greater breadth and at the same time a greater depth—Stake approvingly citing Wolcott: "the trick is to discover essences" (p. 84). And each essence was a particular thing. "Description," it seemed, was anything but simple and everything but surface.

This descriptive space presented a number of dilemmas:

- The space had breadth *and* depth, unavailable to conventional disciplinary knowledge (such as the "experimental psychologist," "the pre-ordinate evaluator," Stake, 1975, p. 21).
- Complexity was assumed rather than established. The researcher had to "preserve" it (p. 12), but without "over- or under-interpreting" (p. 131).
- It was a "case," that is a "bounded system" (p. 47) and at the same time a "holism" (p. 25). The evaluator had both to find it and to put it there.
- Each case was in an "infinitely complex" relation (p. 33) with its context. It was itself only in relation to that constituting "other."
- Its "phenomena" were "fluid and elusive" (p. 33).
- It had to be represented as a "vicarious" experience (Stake, 1975, p. 23) for the reader.
- The account had to "help the reader discern typicality" (Stake, 1995, p. 53), and address competing claims, such as "palatability" (p. 115).
- It must help readers "discover ideas" (Stake, 1995, p. 36), and at the same time discover themselves: "realizing their own consciousness" (p. 41).
- The case had to mix utility and representation, but with a priority for "usefulness" (Stake, 1975, p. 14).
- And the case had to speak the language of the reader—the same "attending and conceptualizing styles similar to those which members of the audience use" (Stake, 1975, p. 23; see also 1995, p. 126), while struggling "to liberate the reader from simplistic views and illusions" (Stake, 1995, p. 99).

The verbs of the first five items (be, have) point to an existence always in tension with the purposefulness of the last five (must, have to). The case had to "be." But also to "behave."

This, then, is the paradoxical space of "responsiveness." It is a space that drew on measures of constructivism ("a creating of meaning," Stake, 1995, p. 136), as well as on a conflicting residual realism expressed in the rhetorics and metaphors of method (for example, the pre-givenness of "complexity," the "discovery" of ideas). It offered an occasional element of a "critical" theory that would demystify ("liberate") readers, via a transparent epistemology of "vicariousness" that returned to the positivist origins of the descriptive space: "conveying to the reader what experience itself would convey" (p. 39). Yet it acknowledged that "case study is subjective, relying heavily on our previous experience and our sense of worth of things" (p. 134). At the same time it constructed itself as an anti-discipline, mediating between the actors' constructions of reality ("negotiation"), and educating them, while still enabling them to "form their own judgments" (p. 28), since they were "often more familiar with the cases" (p. 86)—overall, relying on the actors in a Habermasian kind of way to come to understand each other's viewpoint.

This paradoxical space of description can be presented as wildly eclectic. The "case" was constructed in its complexity via a methodology that posited the invisible as the "transparent," and always the paradoxical. It was an Emperor's clothes methodology, offering its own version of a "magic realism" as the evaluator conjured complexity out of the research hat, while appearing to do nothing at all, representationally, insofar as the task was presented as mere "facilitation" or "naturalistic generalization" (Stake, 1995, p. 36). Yet appearances were deceptive. The simplicity of naturalistic generalization and the convenient separation of "particularization" from "generalization" (p. 8: compare fact/value again) hid the underlying construction of the "case" (any case) as a mix of what we might pair off as necessary couplets: "naturalistic generalization" and "generalistic particularization." What was obscured by burying the latter process was that "the general" informed and constructed "the singular" just as much as the other way round: singularities exist as instances of the general—no "tree" without "trees" and so forth. Yet Stake's rhetoric reflected the pre-givenness of the singularity, its uniqueness, the possibility of "coming to know" what was already there in its "particularity": "Particularization is an important aim, coming to know the particularity of the case" (Stake, 1995, p. 39). Stake seemed to acknowledge that the devil is in the detail, but not that the detail is (always already) in the devil.

In such a scenario, the researcher retained power even while giving it away, abdicating methodology, orchestrating instead something that might more accurately be called truth-seeking "social process," and at the same time building and privileging description with the hidden wand of "generalistic particularization." The obscured nature of such "description" guaranteed the evaluator the "professional" space within which to exert authority, while at the same time appearing not to—through offering an appeasing participation to the "audience." In this way, the evaluator conjures a democratic dove from the silk handkerchief of "naturalistic generalization." The audience may judge, and may choose to applaud. But like all performers, the evaluator is split in that instant between a number of competing appearances and allegiances—open, closed, political, apolitical, theoretical, practical—whatever may be done to attempt to create coherence, or a singular account of an appropriate role performance. Such a *sincere* performance is not on the cards. Little wonder then that the strain would sometimes show: "The chameleon too is something of a role model" (Stake, 1995, p. 104).

And so too is the magician. These fissures should not be read, however, as disabling incompatibilities—in need of remedy, homogenization. Or at least they are not most interesting as such, because they also enable the possibility of the text's overall coherence: "The fissures that divide any text are actually folds that bind them to that which appears to be outside them, and it is precisely these folds that constitute the texts as such, producing the very sense of an inside and an outside that they subvert" (Wigley, 1995, p. 5).

Deconstruction is "the art of the system," "a reflection on the system, on the closure and opening of the system" (Kamuf, 1995, p. 212). It is not difficult, of course, to criticize Stake's methodology as eclectic (if one wishes to object to eclecticism). But instead, this chapter seeks to defend—deconstructively—a certain anarchic tendency in Stake's account of model, methodology, and method. Such is present, to an extent, in any methodological writing. The last purpose, then, is to pin down this magic lurking within methodology, that is, to write positively about what is "unspeakable" in such texts—their very impossibility and so the impossibility of their ever successfully professing or confessing. But again, we should be clear about our intention: this means putting in a good word for the "unspoken" Stake.

What is unspeakable in Stake's *Art* is a largely unaddressed tension between *direction* (in the form of theory, principles, procedures, tips, checklists, and the like) and what is called here for want of an appropriate term *indirection*—those references to the ineffable nature of education or the research task. The space of indirection (another "nothing" of course, in methodological terms) is a kind of antinomy (Gil, 1998), and is opened up by Stake even in his early work when he posits the notion of "matrices" only to undermine them immediately in the name of an as yet unarticulated responsiveness: "These boundaries do not need to be distinct. The categories should be used to stimulate rather than to subdivide our data collection" (Stake, 1967, p. 57).

In *Art,* Stake intersperses more conventional and structuring advice with similar acknowledgments and encouragement: "methods books like this one provide persuasions, not recipes" (Stake, 1995, p. 77). Research is a matter of "casting nets" for meanings rather than anything more precise (p. 37). There is a continuing concern for the "critical uniqueness" of events (p. 44) and for the unexpected questions that "pop up" and redirect inquiry (p. 33). The conditions for doing research and the tempo of the activity set up compromises that influence the study in ways not open to methodological or methodical "taming." The fantasy of method is sometimes asserted: "Good research is not about good methods as much as it is about good thinking" (p. 21).

We could go on, but it should be clear that invocations of the problematic, the need for improvisation, the heterogeneity of situations, the individuality of researchers and evaluators are commonplace. They have to be narrated as *extramethodical performances,* based on experience, imagination, predilection, ability, creativity, desire, and the like. What is even more commonplace is the zeal with which these indirections are also contradicted. Thus Stake can write in a quite different register: "All research is a search for patterns, for consistencies" (Stake, 1995, p. 44). And, "Meanings will come from reappearance over and over" (p. 78). "For the evidence most critical to our assertions, we isolate those repetitions and those correspondence tables most pertinent" (p. 78). He also offers what seems to be direct self-contradiction: "De-emphasize the idea that validity is based on what every observer sees, on simple replication" (p. 87).

In short, "direction" vies with "indirection," culminating in the latter's narrative victory (the last word) as a culminating appeal for the *"advocacy"* of *"integrity"* in case study. To repeat: *"and to make, even by its integrity alone, an advocacy for those things we cherish"* (Stake, 1995, p. 136, emphasis added).

Art triumphs. Method loses its methodological warrant. The space between them cannot be closed. This account, indeed, has related a series of such problematic openings and closures. The moment of "countenance" inverted stimulus and response, opening an illusory space between description and judgment. The outcome—in this account an accidental one—served to *"animate"* methodology by shifting it into the realms of social interaction rather than technical representation. The cost was a fragmentation of rationales, the undermining of methodology, and the opening of dangerously eclectic and paradoxical gaps, which left the identity of the evaluator at the same time "transparent" and duplicitous.

In the end the "countenance" of responsive methodology fails in this deconstructive reading of the "model," despite the various face-lifts examined here. So too does the desirability of "a model" (*any* model, *any* countenance) for the practices of educational inquiry. Spaces with a more "variable geometry" are required, attuned to their contexts and tempos.[11] In this reconceptualization, methodologies, models, methods too need to be situated, local, provisional, and *deconstructive* in their responsiveness to the documents within the case, and the case within (and without) the documents. No more room, either, for the "holism" of the case and its alleged "boundedness." Finally, the lively masquerades of qualitative evaluation, with their casts of stakeholders, audiences, actors, facilitators, negotiators in solemn and honest deliberation, seem also an inadequate rescue for the shaky methodologies of educational evaluation. Method never made anything intelligent, nor was consensus or negotiation ever an adequate guarantor of "educational" process. It is time, therefore, to emphasize the *extra-methodical*, to invent *indirections* under the clear understanding that "loopholes are the law" (Wigley, 1995, p. 160), and that some silences may best be regarded as "vociferous" (Fabian, 1996, p. 306). Such a rejoinder to Stake's "responsiveness" is no rejection: it is a reanimation and a continuing creation. "Up to that moment, that is, when art, which was still fundamentally a means of expression, became aware of the *created* share [author's emphasis, and mine] that it had always added to the world it expressed, *at that moment it could turn away from all past and present reality and create from itself its own reality*" (Augé, 1998, p. 242, my emphasis).

Notes

1. The notes in this chapter are offered both as clarification and as continuing postmodern skepticism about utopian inquiry projects, because they reflect ideals rather than realities. One such project is House and Howe's 1999 evaluation statement, in which they take as one of their exemplary postmodernist educational research texts *Educational Research Undone* (Stronach and MacLure, 1997). Despite its strictures, they can't resist tribalizing those they call postmodernists as a Collective Individual, they fail to consider deconstruction as a political act, they confuse hybridity with pluralism, and they insist on all-or-nothing arguments (if relative then nihilistic, if plural then apolitical, if deconstructive then unprincipled, and so forth) so as to construct a caricature. Above all, they replace the fantasy of epistemological representation with an equally improbable utopia of political representation: "the perceptions and interests of all citizens should be included in decision-making about social policy" (House and Howe, 1999, p. 12). They advocate a kind of evaluative knowledge "undistorted by power relationships" (p. xix). House and Howe confess the idealized nature of their prescription—"too idealized to be implemented straightforwardly in the world as it exists" (p. 111). They nevertheless identify "procedures of professional evaluation," which will ensure the "impartiality" (p. 56) that can help give birth to a "*genuine democracy*" where interests can be known, shared, and negotiated (p. 97, emphasis in original). Continuing postmodern skepticism about such utopian projects is advisable, notably because they imply a capitalism whose political expressions can be tamed into such major change by such minor means. "Inclusion," "dialogue," and "deliberation" are worthy enough slogans, but they are not the butterfly wings that will transform global capitalism, whose effects on the political domain they pass over in silence.

2. "Deconstruction" in this account refers to the *temper* of "playful transcription" that Kundera has written about (Kundera, 1995, p. 80). It aims responsibly (which also means responsively in Heidegger's terms; Gasché, 1995, p. 228) to establish new communication. It does so partly through critique of meaning, but also through what Kamuf (1997) has called "*affirmative* deconstruction" (her stress), a critique that opens up the possibility of meaning. That is, impossibility stands in an enabling relation to the possibility of renewed meaning. "Impossibility is not the opposite of the possible; impossibility releases the possible" (Beardsworth, 1996, p. 26). This account, then, seeks to "renew" Stake.

3. "Deconstruction remarks a certain irreducible and constitutive nonreturn of the subject to itself" (Kamuf, 1997, p. 111). This is Derrida's point about "presence": it never quite makes it. Difference intervenes. Yet not arbitrarily because it is the difference

between singularity—"unrepeatable, ungeneralizable, without genre or gender"—and the necessity to meaning of a certain repetition—"to have even the chance of the other's arrival, it must unfold out of its silence and its secret; that is, it must also be repeatable" (p. 117). This space, which denotes the necessary "betrayal" of the text to its ambitions, both closes down and opens up the possibility of meaning. It is not about "inconsistencies" within an argument (say, intra-paradigmatic error) so much as argument *as* inconsistency (say, paradigmatic failure as a necessity). Such inconsistency may be telling when it expresses what the text least wants to address, and provides a possible starting point for deconstruction, the "angle of entry" (p. 104). Kamuf concludes: "deconstruction 'happens' because of the necessarily unfinished and interminable articulation of singularity with the structures of the same" (p. 118).

4. In contrasting new and old in this context much could be made of the ways in which Stake's rejection of the quantitative approach continued to color his depiction of the qualitative. His explications of the qualitative are invariably contrastive. For example, "we qualitative researchers do not confine interpretation to the identification of variables and the development of instruments" (Stake, 1995, p. 8). This theme has been previously addressed in Stronach, 1997, and is therefore deliberately neglected here.

5. Consultations with colleagues—I will not embarrass them by name—have resulted in the suggestion that this allusion is anachronistic in that the slogan actually referred, many years ago, to the Playtex "Cross-your-heart" brand. Apparently, Wonderbras have, unbeknownst to this author, moved on to less mechanical metaphors. I am grateful for this correction, but not for the need for it.

6. House and Howe reject the separability of fact and value. They are "melded together" (1999, p. xv). Instead they posit a "fact-value continuum" running from "brute facts" to "bare values" (p. 7). They concede that most evaluative work deals with the center of that continuum. It is hard to see, however, how this continuum solves the problem they have identified, because each evaluative judgment has to adjudicate a fact/value intermixture. The continuum does not help any single evaluative decision where the evaluator asks, "what is fact and what is value in this instance?" In addition, House and Howe appeal to the "professionalism" of the evaluator and the propriety of the evaluator's actions to address the fact-value problem. Yet such an appeal to the conscientiousness of the professional hides rather than solves the problem (p. 112).

7. This tendency is taken further by Guba and Lincoln in their "fourth generation evaluation," where the evaluation process becomes essentially a process of orchestration. House and Howe have a similar view of evaluation: "evaluators are orchestrators of a negotiation process" (1999, p. 58). But their account puts a very heavy stress on the "professionalism" of the evaluator. To this European outsider, Stake, Guba and Lincoln, and House and Howe, in their varying visions of evaluation as negotiated communication, all offer versions of the American Dream, conjuring a world of evaluation that reflects democratic ideals rather than realities, all the while claiming to be pragmatic and applied. Each of their evaluation models secretes a fantasy of democracy, whether disinterested in ambition or not. Perhaps the problem partly lies with the universal claims made by such models. "As soon as they are constituted as universal, they cease to be analytical and the religion of meaning begins" (Baudrillard, in Poster, 1988, p. 104).

8. Stake pitched the level of "provocation" lower than House and Howe, and much lower than Guba and Lincoln. Still, it is—according to this reading—appropriate to regard his "responsiveness" as the origin of their more politically interventive styles. It was a big step from the technical to the social methodology, and an obvious further step to ask "what kind of social?" as an overtly political question. For Stake, of course, the politics remained implicit. From a deconstructive point of view, each offers a political fable of perfectible communication. In that sense each constructs an anti-politics whose effect is to obscure the actual entanglements of power and knowledge with a Promised Land of more equal exchanges, more diverse voices, more "professional" adjudication. To put it another way, their utopias are forms of distraction rather than attraction.

9. The reflexive problems in this position are enormous and probably insuperable. If description is complex and uncertain, how much more problematic is *significant* self-description? Of course the evaluator can describe something familiar to reader and writer as a "test" of credibility and viewpoint ("relatively incontestable description," Stake, 1995, p. 62), but insofar as who we are determines *behind our back* what we see, the self-describing researcher is lost. Catching oneself out is Favret-Saada's preferred strategy: "to become one's own informant, to penetrate one's own amnesia, and to try to make explicit what one finds unstatable in oneself" (1980, p. 22). But perhaps the best hope is subsequent deconstruction allowing us retrospectively to trace our various trajectories of inquiry and hence those remainders of the "research self." At any rate, there is no convincing answer to Stake's orienting question: "Is the role of the evaluator nicely apparent?" (Stake, 1995, p. 131).

10. According to House and Howe, Stake's view here should be regarded as positivist in that: "the contents of observation could be (and should be) wholly neutral and intersubjective" (1999, p. 63). Naturally, such positions could be shaded by invoking "minimal valuing" as an ideal, as Stake has frequently done in relation to "advocacy" and "promotionalism." As House and Howe note, such an insistence on "descriptive valuing" as opposed to "prescriptive valuing" redecorates rather than recovers the untenable underlying fact/value distinction.

11. That situatedness is as true for *this* text as for any other. It is a *tactic* here to deconstruct Stake in the main text, but to offer a countercritique rather than a deconstruction of House and Howe in the footnotes. Justification of such tactics cannot step outside power-knowledge considerations. Any contribution to "educational research," however, must be able to make reference to its educative intentions, to open up the possibility of new meanings.

References

Augé, M. *A Sense for the Other: The Timeliness and Relevance of Anthropology* (A. Jacobs, trans.). Stanford, Calif.: Stanford University Press, 1998.

Beardsworth, R. *Derrida and the Political.* London: Routledge, 1996.

Bloom, K. "Introduction." In R. E. Stake, *Evaluating the Arts in Education: A Responsive Approach.* Columbus, Ohio: Merrill, 1975.

Derrida, J. "Limited Inc." *Glyph,* 1977, 2, 162–254.

Fabian, J. *Remembering the Present: Paintings and Popular History in Zaire.* Berkeley: University of California Press, 1996.

Favret-Saada, J. *Deadly Words: Witchcraft in Bocage.* (C. Cullen, trans.). Cambridge: Cambridge University Press, 1980.

Gasché, R. *Inventions of Difference: On Jacques Derrida.* Cambridge, Mass.: Harvard University Press, 1995.

Gil, J. *Metamorphoses of the Body: Theory out of Bounds.* (Vol. 12; S. Muecke, trans.). Minneapolis: University of Minnesota Press, 1998.

House, E. R., and Howe, K. R. *Values in Evaluation and Social Research.* Thousand Oaks, Calif.: Sage, 1999.

Kamuf, P. (ed. and trans.). *Points . . . Interviews, 1974–1994 Jacques Derrida.* Stanford, Calif.: Stanford University Press, 1995.

Kamuf, P. "Deconstruction and Feminism." In N. Holland (ed.), *Feminist Interpretations of Jacques Derrida.* University Park: Pennsylvania State University Press, 1997.

Kundera, M. *Testaments Betrayed.* (L. Asher, trans.). London: Faber & Faber, 1995.

Lyotard, J. F. *The Postmodern Condition: A Report on Knowledge.* (G. Bennington and B. Massumi, trans.). Minneapolis: University of Minnesota Press, 1984.

Phillipson, M. *In Modernity's Wake: The Ameurunculus Letters.* New York: Routledge, 1989.

Popham, J. *Educational Evaluation*. Upper Saddle River, N.J.: Prentice Hall, 1975.

Poster, M. (ed.) *Jean Baudrillard: Selected Writings*. London: Polity Press, 1988.

Power, H. *The Audit Society: Rituals of Verification*. Oxford, England: Oxford University Press, 1997.

Stake, R. E. "The Countenance of Educational Evaluation." *Teachers College Record,* 1967, *68*(7), 523–540.

Stake, R. E. *Evaluating the Arts in Education: A Responsive Approach*. Columbus, Ohio: Merrill, 1975.

Stake, R. *Evaluating Educational Programmes: The Need and the Response*. Paris: CERI/OECD, 1976.

Stake, R. *The Art of Case Study Research*. Thousand Oaks, Calif.: Sage, 1995.

Stake, R. "The Fleeting Discernment of Quality." In L. Mabry (ed.), *Evaluation and the Post-Modern Dilemma: Advances in Program Evaluation*. Series Editor, R. Stake. Greenwich, Conn.: JAI Press, 1997.

Strathern, M. (ed.). *Audit Cultures: Anthropological Studies in Accountability, Ethics and the Academy*. London: Routledge, 2000.

Stronach, I. "Evaluation with the Lights Out: Deconstructing Illuminative Evaluation and New Paradigm Research." In L. Mabry (ed.), *Evaluation and the Post-Modern Dilemma: Advances in Program Evaluation*. Series Editor, R. Stake. Greenwich, Conn.: JAI Press, 1997.

Stronach, I. "Crisis, What Crisis? Dissolving the Insoluble Problems in Representing the "Crisis of Representation."" In P. Hodkinson (ed.), *The Nature of Educational Research: Realism, Relativism or Post-modernism?* Manchester, England: MMU Methodology Series 1, 1999a.

Stronach, I. "Shouting Theatre in a Crowded Fire: 'Educational Effectiveness' as Cultural Performance." *Evaluation*, 1999b, *5*(2), 173–193.

Stronach, I., and MacLure, M. *Educational Research Undone: The Postmodern Embrace*. Buckingham, England: Open University Press, 1997.

Tsoukas, H. "The Tyranny of Light: The Temptations and the Paradoxes of the Information Society." *Futures,* 1997, *29*(7), 827–843.

Weber, E. "Introduction: Upside-Down Writing." In P. Kamuf P. (ed. and trans.), *Points . . . Interviews, 1974–1994 Jacques Derrida*. Stanford, Calif.: Stanford University Press, 1995.

Wigley, M. *The Architecture of Deconstruction: Derrida's Haunt*. Cambridge, Mass.: MIT Press, 1995.

IAN STRONACH is research professor of education at the Manchester Metropolitan University and current lead editor of the British Educational Research Journal.

6

Responsiveness is not merely a characteristic of a special methodology for evaluation. It is also an epistemic and moral virtue that signals a particular relation to the social world and a distinctive way of being and knowing within that world.

Responsiveness and Everyday Life

Thomas A. Schwandt

When responsive evaluation was first introduced by Stake ([1973] 1987) as an approach to conducting an evaluation, it was characterized by the fact that it takes the concerns and issues of stakeholding audiences as its point of departure. Stake claimed that a "pre-ordinate" approach to evaluation emphasized program goals, use of objective tests as measures, comparison of performance to standards held by program personnel, and research-type reports. In contrast, a "responsive" approach was oriented more to program activities than program intents. It responded to audience requirements for information, and took account of the different value perspectives held by stakeholders in reporting program success and failure. Stake also emphasized that responsive evaluations were more attuned to "the natural ways in which people assimilate information and arrive at understanding." He suggested that this meant using styles of reporting that conveyed holistic impressions; that revealed the inherent uncertainty and ambiguity that typically accompany any effort to understand the activity, accomplishments, issues, strengths, and shortcomings of a program that was the object of evaluation; and that created vicarious experience for readers, making it possible for readers to combine this understanding with their previous experience so as to reach new "naturalistic generalizations" (Stake and Trumbull, 1982).

In the decades following his introduction of the idea of responsiveness, Stake has continued to pursue a reconciliation of the professional activity of evaluation with our quotidian ways of knowing and doing. I read much of his work as an effort to encourage evaluators to capitalize on our everyday

---

My special thanks to Tineke Abma, Jennifer Greene, Christina Segerholm, and Robert Stake for their helpful criticisms on earlier drafts of this paper.

73

ways of making sense of the value of social and educational programs, rather than to dismiss or disregard those ways as somehow inferior to a social scientific understanding. Stake has repeatedly emphasized that evaluation knowledge of the success or failure of educational programs should not be thought of solely in terms of propositional knowledge. On the contrary, he has argued that evaluation judgment relies heavily on the tacit dimension of knowing, insight, the realm of the felt, apprehensions, silent sympathies, and the like—all of which lend familiarity, depth, and richness to understanding. To portray evaluation knowledge of this kind, he has promoted forms of reporting that appeal to the ways in which participants and stakeholders (indeed, all of us) ordinarily make sense of (our) selves, others, and the world. Thus, Stake (1991) places a premium on the role of the evaluator as interpreter who must have what he called "anthropological sensitivity"—an ability to pay careful attention to the texture and concrete details of people's experiences, their activities over time, and their physical and social surroundings.

This different way of conceiving evaluation practice and its requisite knowledge is accompanied by a different way of understanding the evaluator's responsibility and role, and, more broadly, the very idea of what it means to be rational as an evaluative inquirer. Stake (Stake and others, 1997) argues that the standard for rational behavior as an evaluator is not procedural and criteriological knowledge (that is, following and applying rules and criteria for knowing). Method may be a useful guide, but it is not a sacred prescription. It alone does not produce the findings of evaluation. In place of an exclusive reverence for procedural rationality, Stake seeks to broaden the view of responsible, rational behavior in evaluation to include moral and political speculation, critique, interpretation, dialogue, and judgment.

All this familiar terrain is typically taken principally to be about a particular way of conceiving of evaluation *methodology*: a statement of a coherent set of assumptions, procedures, and methods to be employed as a model for conducting evaluations. As commonly understood, responsive evaluation takes its place alongside a variety of other evaluation models and approaches (for example, experimental studies, program-theory-based approaches, mixed-method studies) now numbering twenty-two according to Stufflebeam's (2001) latest inventory and analysis. This chapter aims to make the case that responsiveness is not simply or even a particular methodology for evaluation. Responsiveness is also (and perhaps primarily) something like an *epistemic and moral virtue*—a particular kind of human excellence that we strive for in our efforts to understand others and the social world. Virtues are acquired human qualities or traits that make up excellence of character. Responsiveness has an epistemic aspect because it is about "knowing" others; it also has a moral dimension because responsiveness—like honesty, courage, justice, kindness, temperance, and so on—is concerned with "what it is good to be" as a human being. As an epistemic and moral virtue, responsiveness is a distinctive capacity for, or way of, interpretively moving about the world that we aim to realize (albeit always imperfectly) in interacting with fellow human beings. Responsiveness is a quality or virtue we strive for in all human endeavors like evaluating, teaching, administering, providing social services, and so on.

I read Stake's ideas about responsive evaluation as an attempt to align the ways we ought to think and act in evaluation practice with the ways we think and act in practices of teaching, service provision, and the like. The key to understanding this alignment is recognizing that responsiveness is a virtue demanded in all human practices. I am not claiming that Stake himself would define responsiveness in this way, but I do think this interpretation is warranted from a reading of his work. In this chapter, the case for responsiveness as a virtue (rather than as a methodological tool or procedure) is extended by explicating the notion with the aid of ideas drawn from the Aristotelian tradition of practical philosophy as elaborated in recent work in hermeneutic philosophy (for example, Bernstein, 1986; Gadamer, 1981; Gallagher, 1992; Kerdeman, 1998; Smith, 1997; Taylor, 1995; Toulmin, 1988).

The Phenomenology of Responsiveness

There is affinity between responsiveness as a way of knowing in evaluation and what Aristotle described as *phronesis*. Aristotle was concerned with explicating the knowledge required for the particular kind of human activity called *praxis*—a distinctive type of human activity concerned with one's conduct in ethical-political life and requiring its own intellectual commitments and knowledge and its own moral demands (see, for example, Gadamer, 1981). Within the Aristotelian tradition, all ethical, political, and educational activities were regarded as forms of *praxis*. These activities were distinguishable from other forms of human activity defined as *poiesis*. *Poiesis* is a species of rule following or instrumental action. It is the kind of activity found in making things, in the work of craftsmen. *Phronesis* (practical competence, wise judgment) is the knowledge that Aristotle claimed is required for *praxis*. It is the knowledge necessary to moving about as an interpretive being, confronting circumstances that call for deciding what is the appropriate and effective thing to do in the situation at hand. *Poiesis* had its own characteristic form of knowledge as well, called *techne*. This is technical knowledge or expertise grounded in knowing how to use methods, procedures, and rules to bring some specific product into existence.

Both *phronesis* and responsiveness exhibit a characteristic existential structure—they are oriented to *praxis*, flexible, normatively attentive, and concerned with wise judgment.

Orientation to *Praxis*. As noted, *praxis* (practice) is about our "concernful dealings" with one another, as Heidegger once put it (McNeill, 1999).[1] It is about our effort to do the right thing and do it well in our everyday interactions with one another. Taylor (1989) adds that practice is "a stable configuration of shared activity whose shape is defined by a certain pattern of do's and don'ts. The way we discipline our children, greet each other in the street, determine group decisions through voting in elections, and exchange things through markets are all practices. And there are practices at all levels of human life: family, village, national politics, rituals of religious communities, and so on" (p. 204).

There are practices of teaching, public administration, nursing, providing social services, evaluating, and so on. Practices of all kinds are fluid, changeable, and dynamic. They are characterized by their alterability, indeterminacy, and particularity (Pendlebury, 1995). Practices are mutable because they change over time, not simply on a large scale within institutions that sustain and support them, but on a small scale in the daily dealings of an evaluator with a program manager, a social worker with a client, a doctor with a patient, or a teacher with a student. Practices are indeterminate because choices of the appropriate and effective action to take in these "concernful dealings" arise within specific situations and thus are contextually relative. Resources, personal capacities, expectations, obstacles and constraints, and the like are unique to situations. Consider for example, the same practical question as faced by a doctor in a resource-rich suburban clinic and a doctor working in a remote village. In the context of teaching, Pendlebury (p. 60) explains that "a teacher in a well-equipped suburban school with a strongly established academic culture has very different choices open to him or her than a teacher in an ill-equipped, overcrowded ghetto school where the culture of learning has been thoroughly undermined by poverty and political disenchantment." Finally, practices are particular because they are about making correct decisions in consideration of *this* case, *this* person, at *this* time and place, in *this* set of circumstances.

Responsiveness is first and foremost the virtue of being oriented or attentive to *praxis* (practice). It is to recognize that one is dealing with situations that are lived, embodied, experienced, and performed. Stake has expressed this characteristic orientation of responsiveness in evaluation by claiming that evaluation means attending to human practices like teaching or providing social services as contextual experiences—"concernful dealings" of specific kinds that practitioners "undergo" with one another. This is the lived reality of *praxis,* not services provided, programs, projects, or more generically, evaluands.

> What will practitioners heed? They heed stories of people in a plight like their own. They attend to experiential accounts. A good account invites them to recognize the circumstances, never identical to the reader's own, but described in sufficient detail so the reader can decide their similarity and pertinence. . . . Attention to contexts becomes increasingly persuasive. People see their own lives, their own destinies, shaped by immediate contexts: poverty, grace, competition, aspiration, and handicap. They know contexts

shape other lives as well. . . . To understand a program requires knowledge of its contexts, contexts experienced by those who participate. Evaluation is served by experiential accounts. . . . It has become increasingly apparent to me that educators, as most people, work from experiential understandings [Stake, 1991, pp. 76, 81].

Traditionally, researchers have had scant interest in studying the entwining, personalistic, and crisis-like problems of daily practice. Rather, they conceptualize new systems expecting orderly circumstances and dispassionate practitioners. They fiddle with models. But for practitioners, and the helpers of practitioners, the well-being of daily practice is the goal. Sometimes that well-being requires changed practice, sometimes preserved practice, but always practice. The end product desired is not knowledge-about-practice or knowledge-about-subject matter. . . . Practice is guided far more by personal knowings, based on and gleaned from personal experience [Stake and Trumbull, 1982, pp. 7–8].

Flexibility and Normative Attention. Because all practices are mutable and indeterminate, the virtue of responsiveness demands *plasticity*— flexibility in attending to the salient features of each situation. This contrasts with a kind of attention that is directed by templates, procedures, rules, or habits and thus tends to be unmindful of concrete specifics. But "the *salient* features of a situation do not jump to the eye ready labeled for easy identification" (Pendlebury, 1995, p. 60); they must picked out from among the blooming, buzzing confusion of details that comprise any action, person, or event that is the object of our attention. Thus responsiveness requires a particular kind of perspicuity—an ability to discern the relevant features of a case at hand, and this is often spoken of as *normative attention* or *situational appreciation.* What makes attention specifically normative here is its other-regarding character, also referred to as engrossment or an open receptivity to the situation at hand (Noddings, 1992; Nussbaum, 1986). Pendlebury (1995, p. 54) adds that attention is the capacity to "discern with clarity, imagination, and a resonance sustained by emotional involvement" the salient particulars of a situation. In other words, attention is not some easy categorization and description of contextual features as might be based, for example, on checklists, but a "seeing as"—an ability to ascertain what is at stake in this or that circumstance.

   This "seeing as" is analogous to Stake's call for a "social anthropological viewing" on the part of evaluators—an attention to the texture and concrete particulars of everyday life. This kind of "viewing" is often regarded as inferior to the kind of classification and description that is made possible by following a method or a rule. In fact, it is often thought to be a kind of unreliable intuition. The late Isaiah Berlin, however, made the case that the kind of attention spoken of here is hardly "occult and metaphysical, . . . a magic eye able to penetrate into something that ordinary minds cannot apprehend" but rather "something perfectly ordinary, empirical, and quasi-aesthetic in the way that it works" (1996, p. 27). He argues that this kind of attention is a "capacity for integrating a vast amalgam of constantly changing, multicolored, evanescent, perpetually overlapping data, too many, too swift, too intermingled to be caught and pinned down and labeled like so many individual butterflies. . . . To seize a situation in this sense one needs to see, to be given a kind of direct, almost sensuous contact with the relevant data, and not merely to recognize their general characteristics, to classify them or reason about them, or analyze them, or reach conclusions and formulate theories about them" (pp. 27–28).

Moreover, Berlin adds that this kind of attention or engrossment is not what we commonly call *intuition* or (perhaps even more misleadingly) *tacit knowledge*. Rather,

> It is a sense for what is qualitative rather than quantitative, for what is specific rather than general, it is a species of direct acquaintance, as distinct from a capacity for description or calculation or [logical] inference; it is what is variously called natural wisdom, imaginative understanding, insight, perceptiveness, and, more misleadingly intuition (which dangerously suggests some almost magical facility), as opposed to the very different virtues—very great as they are—of theoretical knowledge or learning, erudition, powers of reasoning and generalization. . . . Practical wisdom . . . is a capacity, in the first place for . . . knowledge in the sense in which trainers know their animals, or parents their children, or conductors their orchestras, as opposed to that in which chemists know the contents of their test tubes, or mathematicians know the rules that their symbols obey [p. 28].

Wise Judgment. To have the virtue of *phronesis* or responsiveness means that one is capable of using this perceptive capacity to reach a wise judgment. To grasp the importance of relevant details of a case at hand and to apprehend their interrelationships in human affairs requires the power of discernment; a power that "enables us to discriminate, as discrimination is understood in art, literary, film, or music criticism" (Miller, 1996, p. 225). Discernment or wise judgment requires bringing together two sets of considerations simultaneously into what Pendlebury (1995) calls "perceptive equilibrium." On one hand, one always attends first and foremost to the concrete or situational particulars of the immediate case. On the other hand, one brings into view principles, goods, criteria, standing commitments, and the like. Consider the following example as given by Jonsen and Toulmin (1988): A judge faces a scenario in which the plaintiff testifies in court that she injured herself falling down a defective stairway, which her landlord negligently left unrepaired. Another tenant testifies, to the contrary, that the staircase was not badly maintained and that the plaintiff was drunk at the time of the fall. What is required here in dealing with such a problem? The judgment to be made must first take into account the concrete details of the particular case. In other words, the case itself is always authoritative. At the same time, judgment requires reflecting upon general legal principles, involving here, for example, the probative weight of contrary witnesses. However, no application of a rule, principle, or standing commitment can resolve the matter of how to weigh foreseeable risks and prospective benefits of different courses of action. The issue can only be settled by dialogue between the detailed circumstances of the actual case and respect for general principles.

Or consider the following case, adapted from Pendlebury (1995): a teacher is faced with a decision of what to do with Marie, a ten-year-old student who simply will not do mathematics lessons, even though the child is capable. On one hand, the teacher recognizes that as a teacher she has a standing commitment to cultivate an appreciation of and ability in mathematics in all her pupils. On the other hand, she seeks to "discern with clarity, imagination, and a resonance sustained by emotional involvement" the salient particulars of Marie's situation. She comes to the judgment that Marie is neither willfully disobedient nor simply reluctant but that her life is so filled with family tragedy at the moment that doing mathematics is hardly a priority. The teacher decides that realizing her commitment to what it means to be a good teacher will have to wait until other things are in place for Marie. She does not abandon this standing commitment but interprets in light of her attunement to Marie's situation.

These examples illustrate that responsiveness is not to be mistaken for a kind of spontaneous perception and immersion in particulars. Particulars (the immediate case) are primary, but one cannot discern the conflicts, problems, tensions, issues, strengths, and so on that comprise (and complicate) the effort to reach a judgment without working back and forth between particulars and principles. Thus, responsiveness (*phronesis,* wise judgment) is a unique kind of knowledge precisely because it avoids the extremes of an almost innocent immersion in experience (being awash in a sea of particulars), on one hand, and commitments to general principles, ends, theories, and the like, which are totally blind to fine-grained particularities of the immediate case, on the other.

Stake's account of responsiveness as a way of rendering evaluative judgments resonates with the foregoing picture. In his criticism of Scriven, Stake (Stake and others, 1997) argues that evaluators ought to rely on (and sharpen) their powers of "intuition, quality recognition, and judgment." He contrasts this with Scriven's view that judgment should rely on "rule-governed rationality"—an explicit statement of standards or criteria accompanied by a specific procedure for determining their application. Stake argues that "*perceptual judgment* is the essential logic of evaluation more than is explicit comparison of performance to standards, and efforts to improve professional performance should be to help evaluators judge—not less—but better" (p. 92, emphasis added).

Stake's emphasis on the importance of relying on the insight, clinical inferential ability, practical competence, or wise judgment of evaluators is often read as inferior to rational behavior, for it fails the test of articulating its procedures or criteria. It also has been regarded as an appeal to wholly subjective decision making, a matter of personal taste or preference. But these criticisms fail to acknowledge that the kind of judgment of which Stake speaks as characterizing responsiveness is a kind of knowledge *sui generis*. Critics err in assuming that knowledge generated via procedures and method is the standard or benchmark for what constitutes knowledge or is the only genuine, legitimate evaluation knowledge. The notion that legitimate evaluation knowledge can be expanded to include non-propositional knowledge seems to threaten the very idea of objectivity (and rationality) that lies at the heart of the evaluation enterprise. Likewise, the suggestion that an evaluator best serves as an interpreter who renders tentative portrayals of value challenges the idea of strong summary judgments rendered by evaluation experts and appears to threaten the reduction of evaluation to a matter of individual taste and preference. In much of his work, Stake aims to explain that this is not so. However, what is missing in his argument is an appeal to a long line of thought that makes the case for *phronesis* (wise judgment) as precisely the kind of knowledge necessary to live one's life among one's fellow human beings. This *is* knowledge, and it is of a kind fundamentally different than the knowledge generated via the application of scientific procedure and method.

Moreover, the kind of judgment (practical deliberation) demanded by responsiveness is above all not a simple matter of weigh and sum; it is not calculative as, for example, Scriven suggests it should be in evaluation. Simple weighing assumes that there is some unitary concept of value at stake in a situation calling for a judgment. Pendlebury (1995, p. 63) explains that the person engaged in simple weighing "weighs the alternative courses of action against some measure of the relevant value and chooses the course which will produce the best consequences by maximizing the relevant value at minimum cost. What we have here is an instrumentalist view of practical rationality, in which deliberation is concerned with finding the most effective and efficient means to an end." Scriven's (1992, 1994) qualitative weigh and sum approach to judging program value as a single, unified concept exemplifies this approach. Stake and others (1997) reject this way of framing evaluative judgment in terms of "parsimony, unification, synthesis" and emphasize instead a kind of wise judgment that accounts for "the perspectival, the conditional, and the comprehensive." Stake argues that there is no unitary concept of value (or quality) to be pursued in a given program evaluation. Rather, the "value" of a program is often complex, conditional, uncertain, and manifold. Thus judgment as a matter of rule-based synthesis is replaced by judgment as a narrative account of the recognition of quality. This narrative takes up the personal, social, economic, political, and cultural conditions that affect the perception of the worth or merit of a program. Hence, Stake and others (1997, p. 97) claim, "we do not want our representation of merit to be consistently simpler than the merit really is.

We discourage the use of rubrics which assure a simple picture. We want to describe the complex `values manifold' to be part of the summary report."

Wise Judgment and Narrative Evaluation Accounts. As a mode of rationality, responsiveness demands a species of judgment that is drawn from imaginative questions, sympathetic observation, and openness to the texture of the situation at hand (Pendlebury, 1995). Stake would have us recognize that this kind of judgment is best suited to narrative accounts of value rather than calculation and analysis that yield a final synthesis of value expressed in propositional form. He would have us see that the process of valuing is not exhausted by this kind of measuring. Accordingly, he has called for a form of reporting suitable to capturing lived experience: "We need a reporting procedure for facilitating vicarious experience. We need to portray complexity. We need to convey holistic impression, the mood, even the mystery of the experience. The program staff or people in the community may be uncertain, and the audiences should feel that uncertainty. . . . More ambiguity rather than less may be needed in our reports. Oversimplification obfuscates" (Stake, [1973] 1987, p. 19).

What is not always apparent in this call for a new form of reporting is how responsiveness as a different form of rationality and knowledge *requires* a different way of expressing evaluation judgments. A weigh and sum approach to evaluation inevitably demands a reporting format that clearly displays the procedures employed in calculation (the determination of criteria of merit and their respective weights, the selection of appropriate indicators, the sources and kinds of evidence) and culminates in propositions (statements) reflecting the conclusions of the final synthesis. But this way of speaking and writing about the value of a program is not amenable to a responsive approach grounded in a different way of making practical judgments. Responsiveness on the part of the evaluator entails rendering judgments in a language of qualitative contrasts (Taylor, 1985). This requirement stems from the assumption that our alternative conceptions of value cannot necessarily be expressed in some common units of calculation and thus rendered commensurable. It is a misplaced ambition to turn practical reflection about value as much as possible into calculation. Our understandings of value (quality) entailed in differences between good and bad, right and wrong, base and noble, courageous and cowardly, honest and duplicitous, faithful and treacherous, and so on are rendered contrastively. Each item in any of these pairs can only be understood in relation to the other. Thus, responsive judgment employs a language of evaluative distinctions, not a language of calculation. This language of qualitative contrasts is "most at home and has its most telling exemplars in narratives"; therefore, judgment of lived practice requires narrative redescription: "a story which relates obstacles overcome or still looming large; conflicts resolved, displaced, or deepened; turning points for better or worse; climaxes and culminations" (Pendlebury, 1995, pp. 63–64). It is by means of these carefully crafted accounts or stories that evaluators aim to engage the already elaborately

constructed interpretations of stakeholders and other readers of an evaluation report. The evaluator teaches, not didactically but more in the manner
of an interpreter and perhaps facilitator of inquiry on the part of others. (See
Gallagher, 1992 for a fuller explication of this hermeneutic view of teaching and learning.) More on this last point in the following section.

Some Consequences of Aligning Evaluation with Responsiveness

Stake (1991) has claimed that the greatest challenge in evaluation is helping others understand the complexity of judging the quality of our human
practices. He believes that this problem can be best addressed by realigning
evaluation practice with our ordinary ways of knowing. This realignment is
complex and not without difficulties.

Responsiveness and Critique. Stake generally advocates responsiveness in evaluation because it aims to help practitioners augment
their capacities to judge quality by promoting and enhancing their self-
knowledge. In other words, by being responsive to the case at hand, an
evaluator becomes capable of producing a form of "understanding" quality and value that both resonates with and enhances practitioners' own
faculties to discern and make wise judgments of value. Needing greater
attention here is the matter of the evaluator's obligation to engage in and
encourage the critique of practitioners' own efforts to understand quality. Responsive evaluation may well serve the goal of enlightening practitioners about their beliefs and understandings, but to what extent does
it promote practitioners' critical self-reflection on the possibility that
their discernment and wise judgment may be impaired by irrational
beliefs and misunderstandings? Stake resists assuming responsibility for
this kind of criticism, although he recognizes the difficulty of the choice
(see Chapter One of this volume, and Stake, 2000). In a recent personal
communication (April 2001), Stake further explained the grounds of his
opposition:

> I object to the anticipation of any subsequent evaluator relationship with the
> client or other stakeholder group because it will sometimes discourage full
> critical inquiry into the merit of the evaluand. If evaluators anticipate joining
> into the remediating or training or expediting, they are likely to give greater
> attention during the evaluating to the things they can assist with and less
> attention to the things they cannot. Also, raising certain issues or fault risks
> jeopardizing a follow-up relationship. This redistribution of attention might
> be in the best interests of the client or staff or others, but, in my view, it suf-
> ficiently distorts the basic definition of evaluation to make it objectionable.

Stake wants to establish as clear a line as possible between evaluators'
responsibility for rendering their own accounts and discernments of qual-

ity and their subsequent involvement of any kind with the client or organization. He acknowledges,

> The boundary is not easily placed. The evaluator should consider possible uses of the findings and should not refrain from writing about them. The evaluator should be available after reporting to explain the findings and trim out the implications, that is, to assist in interpretation and answering questions. The contract may explicitly call for dissemination and advice but it should be limited to what is clearly necessary for giving access to the findings/perceptions and not be in effect an offering of subsequent employment or even pro bono consultation.

Moreover, acting as responsive evaluator requires even greater sensitivity to maintaining such a borderline:

> With *praxis* and a qualitative view of evaluation, it is especially true that such a prohibition is needed. It seems that when the parties believe in objective reality, determinative criteria, and management by contingency tables, the evaluator can expect to shy away from personalization of the activity of the evaluand, but a responsive evaluator acclaims the personal view and thus must protect even more against extending personal relationships. It may be more important for the evaluator as person to emphasize service to individuals in need and the society in general, but individuals and society need an institution of evaluation too, where study can be made of merit and worth, without subordination to social action.

Stake argues that responsive evaluators have discharged their responsibility when they have rendered *their own* accounts of the discernment of quality. If well crafted, these narrative accounts serve as portrayals that teach indirectly. They are cases that practitioners can use in educating their self-understandings. A more complete alignment of evaluation with everyday practices entails, I believe, a broader and more direct obligation of evaluators as teachers to promote and develop the capacity for wise judgment in practitioners. I do not regard this as some kind of "subsequent" involvement of the evaluator, but as an integral part of the evaluator's responsibility as a teacher.[2] Borrowing an idea from May (1992), I have called this the obligation to cultivate critical intelligence (Schwandt, 1997a). This entails helping practitioners grasp the rationality of their practices in a broad historical and social context and to examine how ideologies as well as social, political, and economic structures may impede or distort the ability to exercise wise judgment.

In part what complicates defining the obligations of evaluators to deal with issues of involvement and critique are the politics of modern intellectual and professional elites, the formation and maintenance of the institution of evaluation, and the development of democratic communities of practice. Contemporary society is replete with elite consulting practices that claim to have an extraordinary purchase on improving the rationality of everyday life through their access to special knowledge and method. Bauman (1992) has described the intellectual role and social position of these elites in modern society using the metaphor of "legislators of reason." But a call for responsiveness in evaluation that requires evaluators to teach for critical intelligence need not mean the formation of a new legislative elite. And the integrity of the institution of evaluation need not be compromised by responsiveness as explicated here. However, it is likely that the cultural authority of such an institution would no longer rest in the typical scientific rationale for providing a third-party judgment of quality but in its capacity to serve as a teaching institution—one that teaches about making wise judgments. Addressing the complexity of this issue is beyond the purposes of the present chapter. However, to the extent that we relinquish the belief in an authoritative standpoint from which to judge the world and the value of our actions and embrace instead the plurality, ambiguity, uncertainty, contingency, and the endlessly self-critical character of such efforts, we are likely to see the question of the authority of elites and professional practices (including teaching) in a very different light.

Responsiveness and the "Science" of Evaluation. Traditionally, evaluation practice is modeled as a form of modern science that requires craft knowledge and technical expertise to generate explanations of the social world. To use Aristotle's language as noted earlier, it is a human activity called *poiesis*. It is a kind of instrumental action requiring technical knowledge that is used to produce an object; in the present case, that object is an "evaluation" and the accompanying "knowledge of the evaluand" stated in some propositional form. To improve *their* respective practices of teaching, managing, providing social and health care services, and so forth, practitioners are encouraged to accept and implement this knowledge. In other words, judgments of the quality of human actions—for example, Is this a good program? Should these clients be served in this way? Is this an effective teaching method? Is this the best policy for dealing with employees?—are themselves defined as technical problems that have solutions that can be informed by the scientific knowledge provided by evaluators. Thus there is a symbiotic relationship between evaluation as a technical and instrumental undertaking and practices of teaching, public administration, social service provision, and the like, themselves conceived as technical and instrumental tasks.

Efforts to reposition evaluation practice within the ways of everyday knowing and being challenge this picture by arguing that "wise practice" in both evaluation and in practices of teaching, providing social services, and so on requires a different kind of knowledge and associated justification. Traditionally, evaluation knowledge is essentially *conceptual*—the certainty or conviction one has about this knowledge lies in the structure and strength of its argument governed by rules, principles, and methods. Stake, however, promotes the view that the knowledge that evaluation *ought* to generate (because it is the kind of knowledge that practitioners require for good practice) is *perceptual*, not conceptual. Stake's claim is something like this: To judge whether an action is appropriate and effective (in other words, to determine the quality or value of that action), one must be able to perceive and discriminate the relevant details of the situation at hand. These details "must be seized in a confrontation with the situation itself, by a faculty that is suited to confront it as a complex whole" (Nussbaum, 1986, p. 301). The certitude or conviction of this faculty of judgment and discrimination lies in knowledge of particulars and not in knowledge of general principles or methods (Jonsen and Toulmin, 1988).

Elevating the importance of responsiveness as a unique kind of knowledge necessary for evaluation practice does not necessarily mean abandoning the concern with technical knowledge. Stake has made it clear that the "science" of evaluation—its understandings of procedure, methods for generating and collaborating evidence, bias control, and the like—still matter: "By downplaying formalization in general, we are not entitled to a free ride—disciplined judgment becomes all the more critical" (Stake and others, 1997, p. 99). In a recent personal communication, Stake expressed it this way: "Evaluation strategy should not be the replacement of common sense but the disciplining of it." Disciplining judgment and interpretation means that procedures of member checking, meta-evaluation, peer review, and so on ought to be employed in the criticism and refinement of our efforts to discern and portray quality. But, of course, these various procedures are themselves "practical" rather than technical, requiring the exercise of wise judgment on each occasion in which they are used.

Responsiveness and the "Ambition" of Evaluation. Emphasizing responsiveness as an epistemic and moral virtue is a reminder that judgments of the value of human activities never escape the indeterminacy, situatedness, and contingency of interpretation, no matter how much we appeal to procedural rationality, analytic strategies, and objective methods. "Indeterminacy of interpretation" here is not meant in some weak fallibilistic epistemological sense that all knowledge is necessarily uncertain, incomplete, and partial but in a stronger existential sense—we are self-interpreting, meaning-making beings, and the task of interpreting the value of our activities and actions is always contingent, always complex, always contested, never finished.

Recognizing the centrality of responsiveness tempers the scientific ambitions of evaluation practice and suggests a kind of humility about this enterprise as a professional practice. Evaluation exhibits the same characteristics of all human practices. Yet the common belief is that because of its reliance on formalized methods, evaluation practice can claim a special purchase on questions of the quality (value) of other human practices. The dichotomous thinking that characterizes virtually all of Western thought leads us to the mistaken belief that the only alternative to a science of evaluation is intuitive understanding, individual taste, and personal preference. Where this kind of thinking prevails, responsiveness as a way of knowing and interpretively moving about the social-political world will always be regarded as, at best, an inferior intellectual capacity, completely ill-suited for use as the foundation of a scientific practice of evaluation, and of course without merit as a professional service that can be sold to clients. Stake's explication of responsiveness in evaluation is one way of defining a middle ground between this either-or thinking: between overreliance on and overapplication of method, general principles, and rules to making sense of ordinary life on one hand, and advocating trust in personal inspiration and sheer intuition on the other. Stake makes a case for the restoration of responsiveness as another legitimate way of "doing" evaluation. In his call for attending to the multilayered qualities of lived experience and rendering a wise judgment of the ways in which these qualities are manifest in a particular program or project he is telling a cautionary tale. It is a tale that reminds us that judgments of the value of our practices are always incomplete, unsettled, and, if well done, not scientifically authoritative but generative of further interpretive deliberations about the ends and means of the practices themselves.

Notes

1. The terms *praxis* and *practice* are often used interchangeably, but the two carry quite different meanings. The significance of the modern use of the word *practice* is typically determined by its connotations in connection with the application of theory and science to everyday life. In contemporary definitions, theory is the realm of thinking or reflecting and practice is the realm of doing or acting. Theory and practice are defined oppositionally, and practice is everything that theory is not. Thus we hear talk of evaluation theory as something different from evaluation practice, or a theory of teaching as opposed to the practice of teaching. The Greek term *praxis* (although used in several different ways by Aristotle), however, is not related to a theory-practice distinction. *Praxis* is a distinct type of human activity distinguishable from *poiesis*. One can have a theory of *praxis* and a theory of *poiesis*.

2. I have argued elsewhere for an evaluation obligation that is "value-critical" but not "value-committed" (Schwandt, 1997a, 1997b, 1997c, forthcoming)—aiming to steer a middle ground between illumination and enlightenment on one hand, and championing specific norms and causes on the other (see also Carr, 1995).

References

Bauman, Z. *Intimations of Postmodernity.* London: Routledge, 1992.

Berlin, I. "On Political Judgment." *New York Review of Books,* Oct. 3, 1996, pp. 26–30.

Bernstein, R. J. "From Hermeneutics to Praxis." In B. Wachterhauser (ed.), *Hermeneutics and Modern Philosophy.* Albany: State University of New York Press, 1986.

Carr, W. *For Education: Towards Critical Educational Theory.* Buckingham, England: Open University Press, 1995.

Gadamer, H-G. *Reason in the Age of Science.* (F. G. Lawrence, trans.). Cambridge, Mass.: MIT Press, 1981.

Gallagher, S. *Hermeneutics and Education.* Albany: State University of New York Press, 1992.

Jonsen, A. R., and Toulmin, S. *The Abuse of Casuistry.* Berkeley: University of California Press, 1988.

Kerdeman, D. "Hermeneutics and Education: Understanding, Control, and Agency." *Educational Theory*, 1998, *48*(2), 241–266.

May, W. F. "The Beleaguered Rulers: The Public Obligation of the Professional." *Kennedy Institute of Ethics Journal*, 1992, *2*(1), 25–41.

McNeill, W. *The Glance of the Eye: Heidegger, Aristotle, and the Ends of Theory*. Albany: State University of New York Press, 1999.

Miller, R. B. *Casuistry and Modern Ethics: A Poetics of Practical Reasoning*. Chicago: University of Chicago Press, 1996.

Noddings, N. *The Challenge to Care in Schools*. New York: Teachers College Press, 1992.

Nussbaum, M. *The Fragility of Goodness: Luck and Ethics in Greek Tragedy and Philosophy*. Cambridge, England: Cambridge University Press, 1986.

Pendlebury, S. "Reason and Story in Wise Practice." In H. McEwan and K. Egan (eds.), *Narrative in Teaching, Learning and Research*. New York: Teachers College Press, 1995.

Schwandt, T. A. "Evaluation as Practical Hermeneutics." *Evaluation*, 1997a, *3*(1), 69–83.

Schwandt, T. A. "The Landscape of Values in Evaluation: Charted Terrain and Unexplored Territory." In D. J. Rog and D. Fournier (eds.), *Progress and Future Directions in Evaluation: Perspectives on Theory, Practice, and Methods*. New Directions for Evaluation, no. 76. San Francisco: Jossey-Bass, 1997b.

Schwandt, T. A. "Whose Interests Are Being Served? Evaluation as a Conceptual Practice of Power." In L. Mabry, (ed.), *Evaluation and the Post-Modern Dilemma: Advances in Program Evaluation*. Series Editor, R. Stake. Greenwich, Conn.: JAI Press, 1997c.

Schwandt, T. A. *Evaluation Practice Reconsidered*. Baltimore, Md.: Peter Lang, forthcoming.

Scriven, M. "Evaluation and Critical Reasoning: Logic's Last Frontier?" In R. A. Talaska (ed.), *Critical Reasoning in Contemporary Culture* (pp. 353–406). Albany: State University of New York Press, 1992.

Scriven, M. "The Final Synthesis." *Evaluation Practice*, 1994, *15*, 367–382.

Smith, N. H. *Strong Hermeneutics: Contingency and Moral Identity*. London: Routledge, 1997.

Stake, R. E. "Program Evaluation, Particularly Responsive Evaluation." Keynote address at the conference "New Trends in Evaluation," Institute of Education, University of Göteborg, Sweden, Oct., 1973. In G. F. Madaus, M. S. Scriven, and D. L. Stufflebeam (eds.), *Evaluation Models: Viewpoints on Educational and Human Services Evaluation*. Boston: Kluwer-Nijhoff, 1987.

Stake R. E. "Retrospective on 'The Countenance of Educational Evaluation.'" In M. W. McLaughlin and D. C. Phillips (eds.), *Evaluation and Education: At Quarter Century. Ninetieth Yearbook of the National Society for the Study of Education, Part II*. Chicago: University of Chicago Press, 1991.

Stake, R. E. "A Modest Commitment to the Promotion of Democracy." In K. E. Ryan and L. DeStefano (eds.), *Evaluation as a Democratic Process: Promoting Inclusion, Dialogue, and Deliberation*. New Directions for Evaluation, no. 85. San Francisco: Jossey-Bass, 2000.

Stake, R. E., and others. "The Evolving Syntheses of Program Value," *Evaluation Practice*, 1997, *18*(2), 89–104.

Stake, R. E., and Trumbull, D. J. "Naturalistic Generalizations." *Review Journal of Philosophy and Social Science*, 1982, *7*(1–2), 1–12.

Stufflebeam, D. L. *Evaluation Models*. New Directions for Evaluation, no. 89. San Francisco: Jossey-Bass, 2001.

Taylor, C. *Philosophical Papers*. Vol. 1: *Human Agency and Language*. Cambridge, England: Cambridge University Press, 1985.

Taylor, C. *Sources of the Self: The Making of the Modern Identity*. Cambridge, Mass.: Harvard University Press, 1989.

Taylor, C. *Philosophical Arguments*. Cambridge, Mass.: Harvard University Press, 1995.

Toulmin, S. "The Recovery of Practical Philosophy," *American Scholar*, 1988, *57*(3), 345–358.

THOMAS A. SCHWANDT *is professor of education at the University of Illinois at Urbana-Champaign, where he holds appointments in the Department of Educational Psychology and the Unit for Criticism and Interpretive Theory.*

Parallels are drawn between responsive evaluation of program quality and personalized assessment of individual learning. The commonalities emphasized include attention to uniqueness, respect for local understandings and contexts, and promotion of meaningful agency.

Responsive Evaluation Is to Personalized Assessment . . .

Linda Mabry

This chapter offers consideration of the relationship between a responsive approach to the evaluation of educational programs and a personalized approach to the assessment of student achievement. A personalized approach to assessment evaluates the quality of the unique accomplishments of individual students. Using discussion and analogy to engage propositional and metaphoric meaning-making, responsiveness as a motif for inquiry about both program quality and student accomplishment is explored. The discussion is pursued through a series of relational juxtapositions: the relationship between achievement testing and program evaluation, between standardized test scores and student achievement, between personalized assessment and student achievement, and between personalized assessment and responsive program evaluation.

The Relationship Between Achievement Testing and Program Evaluation

Achievement test scores are to *evaluations of educational programs* as

(a) Hello is to a conversation
(b) The punchline is to a joke
(c) A mask is to a Halloween costume
(d) The line is to a line drawing

Are test scores a beginning point for the evaluation of an educational program, an introductory hello, or a final clinching argument, the data that deliver the final punch? Are test scores optional for evaluations of educational programs as either makeup or a mask may be used in a disguise, or are they as essential as the line is to a line drawing?[1]

A few years ago, I was invited to propose an evaluation to the Board of Education of an Indiana school district considering whether to remodel some local school buildings. They wanted to know whether their open classrooms, built in the 1960s, provided optimal physical environments for the pedagogical strategies in use thirty years later. In our first telephone conversation, the superintendent assured me the district had data I would find useful—scores from standardized student achievement tests.

Whether test scores had risen, declined, or remained about the same across time, I marveled that he thought they could be informative about the appropriateness of the architecture. The superintendent's confidence that standardized, norm-referenced test scores would function as relevant and even primary data for this purpose vividly exemplifies an enduring public perception that scores on tests designed to measure the achievement of individuals are centrally relevant to evaluations of the educational programs provided to them. This perception flourishes, in part, because of the high importance accorded to student outcomes in education. This perception also flourishes because of misplaced cravings for simple indicators to represent complex phenomena. Clearly, educational programs are highly complex, and individual student test scores can only capture a fraction of this complexity. Yet educational accountability schemes continue to prioritize test scores as critical indicators of educational quality.

Program evaluators, too, have sometimes prioritized standardized, norm-referenced achievement test scores as the ultimate measures of program quality. However, many evaluators have rejected overreliance on single indicators of program quality and heeded admonitions in the *Standards for Educational and Psychological Testing* (American Educational Research Association, American Psychological Association, and National Council on Measurement in Education, 1999) against using tests for purposes for which they have not been validated. Scores from tests designed to measure individual achievement but used to represent program achievement have been challenged by evaluators concerned that resultant inferences of program quality will be invalid and the usefulness and value of their evaluations undermined. Because *most* tests of individual student achievement are not designed or validated as measures of school quality (Koretz, 2001), scores are not an adequate or appropriate basis for evaluating a school's educational program, nor are they likely to promote valid inferences of quality.[2]

Moreover, the tests are technically flawed. Scores always include measurement error, the sources and magnitude of which can only be estimated. Charges of bias surface and resurface. State tests are poorly aligned to state content standards, and performance standards are shockingly arbitrary (Boser, 2001; Elmore and others, 2001; Goertz, 2001; Kane, 1994). So, for evaluators, it is doubly problematic to base educational program evaluation on aggregated individual scores. Still, prioritization of test scores as indicators of important outcomes is apparent in evaluation approaches conducted primarily for policy audiences, for example, econometric evaluations.

In counterpoint, responsive evaluation, developed and described by Robert Stake ([1973] 1987, 1975; see also Abma and Stake's presentation in Chapter One of this volume, and Stake and Pearsol, 1981), is one approach to evaluating educational programs that rejects test scores as primary indicators of educational quality. The characteristics of responsive evaluation are orthogonal to standardized, norm-referenced multiple-choice achievement testing. Where responsive evaluation features emergent design, standardized testing employs pre-ordinate design—predetermined decisions about the content and format of test items, potential answers, number of items, levels of item difficulty, time to complete the test, and range of scores. Shunning prescriptiveness, responsive evaluation's heuristic data collection and its inductive, intuitive interpretation contrast with (and imply criticism of) the formulaic procedures of standardized achievement testing.

Responsive evaluation and standardized testing differ also regarding intended use of results and political authority. Responsive evaluation promotes understanding of unique achievements and progress over time, of a school's singular contexts and accomplishments regarding curriculum, pedagogy, working relationships, climate, and progress. Standardized test scores offer very limited understanding of a child's achievement or a school's accomplishments. In contrast to the centralized, often external mandate for standardized testing, responsive evaluation redistributes authority, ceding to stakeholders the right and responsibility for formulating evaluation interpretations, which some critics consider to be a truncation of professional responsibility (see Scriven, 1998). Whether the fulcrum for evaluation should be stakeholder judgment or evaluator judgment depends on one's stance regarding appropriate locus of program authority and expertise—practical wisdom versus the professionalism of the guild (Smith, 1998).

The Relationship Between Standardized Tests and Student Achievement

Content Validity. A standardized test's *content* (for example, the items on a math test) is to the test's *academic domain* (for example, mathematics) as

(a) An apple is to all the fruit in the orchard
(b) A map is to the terrain
(c) The items in a grocery basket are to the items in the grocery store
(d) A timeline is to historical events

Do the items on a test adequately sample the domain? Are all the items on a math test relevant to mathematics and, as a group, fully representative of math—a microcosm of the domain, as an apple is to the orchard? Is the test a representation of the domain, which is distorted by technical limitations, as a two-dimensional map is to a three-dimensional geographic area? Is test content a subsidiary inventory distorted by subjective choice, as a shopper's selection of purchases is to the store's inventory? Is the test a minimal outline of the whole, as a timeline is to history?

Much standardized test construction and scoring better ensure that scores can be ranked than that the domain is well represented by the test items. A standardized, norm-referenced, multiple-choice achievement test typically begins with a table of specifications, a matrix pairing topics with item difficulty level. In developing and selecting items, those that discriminate between high-performing and low-performing test-takers are preferred because standard scores, which will represent distances from the average score or norm, must spread out. Preference for items that discriminate among test-takers, rather than for items relevant to and representative of the content domain, tends to constrict test content inappropriately, as when a multifaceted subject is reduced to a few homogeneous test items because those items are sufficient to differentiate test-takers' performances. Thus test content often represents academic domains poorly.

Subjective decisions occur at many points in the development of so-called objective tests: determinations of item types, topics, difficulty, number, wording, order of appearance on the test, foils. Human choice determines which test to use, whether to develop a test or to select an off-the-shelf exam. Standardized testing does not substitute objective measurement for subjective teacher assessments but substitutes test developers' subjective judgments for teachers' subjective judgments. If content is not particularly well represented in standardized, norm-referenced achievement tests, consider how well these tests can measure student achievement.

Valid Inferences of Achievement. A *student's score* on a standardized achievement test is to that *student's knowledge and skill* in the content area of the test as

(a) A thermometer reading is to the person's temperature
(b) An autobiography is to the author
(c) A photograph in a yearbook is to the high school experiences of the student portrayed
(d) An address is to the person who resides there

Is a test score as accurate a measure of a person's achievement as a thermometer reading is of a person's temperature? Is a test score intentionally produced by the test-taker in the way an autobiography is intentionally produced by the author? Is a test score, as a way to locate a student's performance among those of an age group, as descriptive and particular as an address? Or is a test score a snapshot of a nervous moment frozen in time? Manhattan federal judge John M. Walker produced foil (c) in the analogy item above. In a suit brought by American Civil Liberties Union Women's Rights Project, Walker ruled against New York State's method of granting merit scholarships based on scores from standardized, norm-referenced, multiple-choice college entrance examinations. In rendering a decision that the standardized tests discriminated unfairly, he stated: "After a careful review of the evidence, this court concludes that S.A.T. scores capture a student's academic achievement no more than a student's yearbook photograph captures the full range of her experiences in high school" (Glaberson, 1989, p. 1).

Walker's ruling illustrates the vast distance between common meanings and test developers' notions of *discrimination*, described earlier. *Norm-referenced tests* composed of items that merely discriminate among test-takers, denying them opportunity to demonstrate what they know and can do, fail to solicit what they have achieved.

Achievement tests that serve to rank students more than to measure their achievements suggest several cautions for evaluators considering a heavy reliance on standardized tests in their educational evaluations. First, standardized norm-referenced testing would be problematic in evaluation even if test scores represented test-takers' achievements well. Norm-referencing leads to descriptions of the achievements of half of all test-takers as below average, suggesting the capacity to injure self-esteem and to depress aspiration and motivation. Surely achievement tests should not depress achievement; surely educational evaluation should not contribute to threats to student achievement. Second, norm-referenced scores are relative distances from the average or norm, and those students scoring below the norm will be told their performances are below average *even if their performances indicate proficiency*. Invalid inferences and actions hurtful to students and programs may well result from reports that proficient performances are below average.

Finally, standardized testing is by design insensitive to local teaching. Students exposed to curricula better aligned to test content and format have a better chance at high scores. Differential test preparation guarantees inequity. For evaluating programs, high scores that appear to be evidence of program quality may actually reflect the alignment, perhaps improper or even illegal, between tests and curriculum and pedagogy (Haladyna, Nolen, and Haas, 1991). Strong test preparation is not always strong educational practice. Tests that narrow the curriculum to easily tested topics and that encourage so-called multiple-choice teaching can undermine education and, as indicated, educational evaluation.

Alternatives to Norm-Referenced Standardized Multiple-Choice Testing. Assessments of student achievement need not be norm-referenced or standardized or limited to multiple-choice items. Alternatives to norm-referenced tests—*criterion-referenced tests* and *standards-based tests,* now in vogue—compare student performances not to a norm but to criteria or standards, respectively. In theory, comparison to a criterion or standard allows the achievement of all test-takers who meet the external referent to be described as proficient, not just the top half. But, in practice, performance criteria and standards often reflect normative expectations or data (see, for example, Impara and Plake, 1997; Popham, 1995). Consequently, the problems of norm-referenced testing described here are not isolated to norm-referenced tests.

The movement toward *performance assessment,* an alternative to multiple-choice testing, has been so influential that all but three states now include constructed-response items in their testing systems (Boser, 2001). But standardized performance assessments can produce distortions in curriculum and pedagogy similar to the distortions of standardized multiple-choice tests. Curricula can narrow either to topics easily tested by multiple-choice items or to the types of constructed responses required on standardized performance assessments. Pedagogy can be distorted to teaching to the test or to writing to the rubric (see Hillocks, 1997; Mabry, 1999b).

Curriculum-based assessment, responsive to the classroom curriculum, is more likely than a standardized test to indicate whether students have learned the material provided specifically to them. For program evaluation, curriculum-based assessment is less likely than standardized assessment to indicate whether the achievement of students in the program is comparable to the achievement of students elsewhere but is more likely to indicate whether a program has accomplished its purpose. Thus, curriculum-based assessment is clearly useful for goal-based evaluation (see Scriven, 1991, pp. 178–180), but is less clearly useful for detecting unintended programmatic consequences, good or bad.

Assessment can be more responsive to individual students than to norms, external criteria or standards, or the delivered curriculum. It can be more responsive to students' individual styles of self-expression than multiple-choice items or standardized performance assessments. Personalized student assessment can be sensitive to individual students in a manner analogous to the sensitivity to individual programs of responsive evaluation.

The Relationship Between Personalized Assessment and Student Achievement

A *personalized assessment* of achievement is to a *student's knowledge and skill* as

(a) A pine cone is to an evergreen forest
(b) A clock is to time
(c) A self-portrait is to the artist
(d) The price of a house is to the owner's home improvements

Could a personalized assessment of a student's achievement belong to any student in the class (or school or country); could a pine cone have come from any tree in the forest? Is personalization a tool for breaking down the amorphous construct *achievement* into measurable gradations in the way a clock measures time in hours and minutes? Does personalizing assessment mean giving the student the authority to decide when and how to represent current knowledge and skill, tantamount to taking the brush and canvas from the tester and giving it to the test-taker? Is a personalized assessment an external indicator of a student's academic progress, as a listing price indicates a real estate agent's assessment of a property and its improvements?

Personalization is an approach to assessment that directs focus toward individual students and their unique accomplishments (Mabry, 1999a). Personalized assessment may—or may not—become the latest wave of measurement strategies, each a reaction to the disadvantages of the previous wave:

- Criterion-related and standards-based testing imply critique of norm-referenced testing's rankings of relative student performance, countering that student achievement is better understood by comparison to a standard than by comparison to a norm.
- Performance assessment implies critique of multiple-choice testing's inattention to students' different response styles, countering that student achievement is better understood when the student is allowed to demonstrate accomplishment through original performance rather than forced to select from among the test developer's predetermined multiple-choice foils.
- Curriculum-based assessment implies critique of standardized testing's disregard of classroom curricula, countering that student achievement is better understood in relation to the curriculum the student has actually experienced than in relation to standardized content to which the student will have had uneven exposure at best.
- Personalized assessment implies critique of standardized testing's insensitivity to students as individuals, countering that student achievement is better understood by concentrating on the student's demonstration of knowledge and skill than by concentrating on external expectations that may have little meaning for the student.

In comparing these approaches to assessing student achievement (see Table 7.1), where standardized testing is indifferent to the individuality of a student, and where contextualized (Berlak, 1992) or curriculum-based assessment considers a student's achievement in terms of mastery over the delivered curriculum, personalized assessment focuses on singular achievement. Consistent with constructivist learning theory, personalized assessment involves the evaluation of individuals' unique constructions of knowledge, rather than presuming that all students should know the same things, and typically gives the student a voice in determining the content and skills to be assessed. Consistent with accepted understandings of variation in human development (Erikson, 1963; Kohlberg, 1984; Piaget, 1955; Vygotsky, 1978), personalized assessment does not assume that all students will achieve proficiency

Table 7.1. Approaches to the Assessment of Student Achievement.

	Psychometric approach	Contextual approach[a]	Personalized approach[b]
Test content	Standardized test content regardless of the curricula offered to students	Curriculum-sensitive test content to determine whether a student learned what was taught	Student-sensitive test content adapted to the construction of meaning by an individual student
Test administration	Standardized administration featuring identical test directions, answer formats, availability of resources, and typically time	Administration flexibly adapted for classroom conditions and expectations regarding directions, assistance, resources, and time	Individualized administration in which a student may determine or negotiate the assessment format, materials, starting point and time allowed
Test items	Identical items for all test-takers, externally, often commercially prepared—typically selected-response items (especially multiple-choice), sometimes constructed-response items[c]	Items reflecting the curriculum, identical for all test-takers, which may be commercially or teacher-developed—with teachers' tests more likely to include both selected-response and performance items	Items and item type individualized for each test-taker—typically performance items determined or negotiated by the student
Scoring	Selected-response items typically scored by scantron, constructed-response items typically scored by paid scorers trained to use a rubric to judge student performance	Teacher-scored often using a commercial or teacher-developed answer key or, for constructed-response items, either a rubric or subjective judgment	Teacher-scored and perhaps scored by other faculty, students, and community members using subjective judgment and individualized standards rather than a key or rubric
Self-evaluation	Self-evaluation not offered or considered	Self-evaluation sometimes encouraged	Self-evaluation required as essential to the student's development
Use of results	Summative ranking of scores used to select students for high school graduation, college admittance, special programs, remediation, tracking, retention, and so on	Summative use as grades for units or courses, formative use for curriculum development or instructional planning	Summative use as grades for units or courses or diplomas, formative use for further education and development of the individual student

Note: [a] From Harold Berlak (1992, pp. 1–22), who contrasts the "psychometric paradigm" with the "contextual paradigm," which is more respectful of classroom and curriculum contexts and more resonant with curriculum-based assessment.

[b] From Mabry (1999a, chapter 2) where the "personalized paradigm" is contrasted with both the psychometric and contextual.

[c] *Selected-response items:* Test-takers choose from response options provided on the test. Examples: multiple-choice items, true-false items, matching items, fill-in-the-blank or cloze items where the response options are provided on the test. *Constructed-response items:* Test-takers construct their own unique responses. Examples: essay tests, demonstrations, experiments, research reports, creative writing, oral or musical or dramatic or dance performances.

concurrently but, rather, adjusts for differences regarding the timing of mastery and readiness for assessment. Consistent with the theory of multiple intelligences (Gardner, 1983), personalized assessment provides opportunity for students to demonstrate their achievements in their preferred modes of performance rather than requiring them to respond to standardized test formats.

Personalized assessment is facilitated by assessors' familiarity with the student's academic record, personal background, and interests, which allows consideration of a specific performance in the context of broad understanding of the student's capacity, progress, and goals. The importance of assessor-assessee familiarity suggests that personalized assessment is more operable in classrooms and small schools than on a large scale. Where there are committees of assessors, each would be expected to know the student in a different way and to offer unique feedback based on unique knowledge. Reliable or consistent scoring might be desirable but not at the expense of forced consensus or denial of multiple viewpoints.

The critical viewpoint is the student's in personalized assessment, a recognition that the most important assessments are those made by oneself. Belief in the crucial role of self-knowledge resonates with a value of supporting students as they develop self-evaluation capacity, personal standards of quality, and responsibility for their education and lives. Further, a common complaint leveled against standardized achievement tests, even tests described as diagnostic, is that—test preparation aside—they provide little useful information for student remediation or classroom instruction (Stiggins and Conklin, 1992). While curriculum-based tests are naturally more informative, for teachers interested in maximizing each child's learning opportunity, personalized assessment is even more useful.

Personalized assessment enhances the validity of inferences of a student's achievement by providing opportunity to understand achievement as an individual construction of knowledge and repertoire of skills, an improvement over testing approaches lacking in reference to the student (Mabry, 1995, 1999a). As Stake has observed (1991), "Knowing the rank order of students as to proficiency is not at all the same as knowing what students know. . . . Education is not so much an achieving of some fixed standard. In a true sense, it requires unique and personal definition for each learner. . . . Education is a personal process and a personally unique accomplishment" (p. 7).

The Relationship Between Personalized Assessment and Responsive Evaluation

Personalized assessment is to *responsive evaluation* as

(a) A student is to an adviser
(b) Groucho is to Harpo

(c) Sociology is to anthropology
(d) Ink is to a fountain pen

Is personalized assessment the intellectual offspring of responsive evaluation, or do both spring from a common progenitor and bear a fraternal
resemblance? Is the resemblance between personalized assessment and
responsive evaluation less family-like and more like that of sociology
and anthropology, lines of inquiry with comparable epistemology and
methodology and overlapping interests in human culture and interaction?
Or is the relationship more like that between ink and pen, personalized
assessment supplying informative data for a responsive evaluation of an
educational program?

Oppositional stances in assessment are analogous to the sometimes
oppositional approaches to program evaluation (see Madaus, Scriven, and
Stufflebeam, 1987; Shadish, Cook, and Leviton, 1991; Stufflebeam, Madaus,
and Kellaghan, 2000; Worthen, Sanders, and Fitzpatrick, 1997). In particular, personalized assessment's implied critique of standardized testing's
inflexibility toward individual students is analogous to responsive evaluation's implied critique of pre-ordinate inquiry's inflexibility toward programs
as unique entities.

As responsive evaluation orients to program uniqueness, personalized
assessment orients to an individual's unique knowledge and skills, perspective, background and circumstances, progress over time, interests, and goals.
Orientation toward individuality, understood in context, promotes particularistic and holistic understandings such as recognition that cognitive
growth involves affective, motivational, and conative dimensions and that
students' gains in knowledge and skill occur formally and informally inside
and outside school. Similar to responsive evaluation's alertness to program
context, personalized assessment considers achievement gains in the context of students' differential opportunity and readiness. In this way, personalized assessment has a capacity for equity in assessment unavailable to
standardized assessment.

Personalized assessment's focus on a student's unique achievement
compares with responsive evaluation's focus on a program as a case with its
own purposes and developmental timetable, its unique achievements and
interests and contexts. Both concentrate on the heart of the matter, little dis-
tracted by external criteria or weighting systems (Stake and others 1997) or
rubrics or prescribed scoring procedures (Mabry, 1999b), or by comparison
to other programs or other students. Neither presumes in advance which
aspects will merit attention; both are committed to gaining familiarity nat-
uralistically over time. In the end, both offer information and interpretations considered in context and reserve ultimate judgments to the judged.

Personalized assessment and responsive evaluation are parallel but
related developments in parallel but related fields. Neither derives from the
other; both build upon ordinary ways of understanding applied with intense

focus and systematicity to students or programs, respectively. The similarities are conceptual, epistemological, methodological, and ideological, with practical benefits. Where test scores might be preferred by a cost-benefits analyst, more comprehensive, personalized assessment data might be more credible and useful to a responsive evaluator who would be unlikely to accept aggregated scores as firm evidence of program quality. A responsive evaluator is likely to respect the particularity of individual performances, the perspectives of multiple assessors, and the implications of testing— intended and unintended, positive and negative—for program quality.

Practical Difficulties. Personalized assessment raises difficulties familiar to responsive evaluators: issues of rigor, validity, time, comparative merit, and equity. Is personalized assessment rigorous enough in practice to promote valid inferences of student achievement, or are assessors familiar with the child too sympathetic; is a responsive evaluator too sympathetic to stakeholders? Is there time enough for deep acquaintance with a child or program? Without reference to classmates or agemates, is personalized assessment insufficiently informative; without comparison data from other programs with similar goals, is responsive evaluation insufficiently informative? Do individualized performance standards make personalized assessments too easy for some students and too difficult for others; does evaluation responsive to individual programs hold one to higher expectations than another? Ultimately, the quality of a personalized assessment and of a responsive evaluation depend on the skill and integrity of the assessor and the evaluator.

But, then, *all* assessments and all evaluations depend on the skill and integrity of the practitioner. Personalized assessment and responsive evaluation deny the practitioner external criteria and referents, and they effectively prohibit easy descriptions of evaluative processes and easy justifications for interpretations. Standardized test development and scoring are easily explained and followed—tables of specifications, scoring rubrics, conversions of raw scores into standard scores. But the mental processes for determining appropriate standards for individuals and for judging proficiency based on complex, nonstandard information are decidedly difficult to articulate, especially in advance. Any responsive evaluator who has wondered what to do next, faced potential clients wanting advance description of what they are paying for, or faced stakeholders demanding explanation for data they consider irrelevant or interpretations they disapprove will recognize the heavy demands of judgment-intensivity. Articulation skills are especially needed for personalized assessment and responsive evaluation.

Assessment and Evaluation in the Postmodern Era. But good articulation, even good practice, is not enough these days. Critical theorists and postmodernists unmask hegemony everywhere, denouncing the oppressions of the status quo and its exploiters, its unwitting contributors and beneficiaries, and its complicit victims (see Mabry, 1997). No less suspect than governments and industrialists are social scientists, who now regularly face challenges to data and interpretations. Commissioned studies and whole bodies of empirical literature are questioned or disregarded. Claims of having measured achievement or of knowing a program's quality can be denounced as false grabs for truth and authority. Assessing and evaluating are modern enterprises presuming a truth to be discerned, a way of getting at it, an expertise to exert—delusional power ploys in the postmodern era.

Personalized assessment and responsive evaluation are trapped in postmodern condemnation but not at the bottom of the pit. Neither imposes external criteria; rather, both accept uniqueness and attempt to adapt appropriately and sensitively. Neither forces the judgment of the expert; rather, both elevate lay opinion. More dispersals of authority than exercises in centralized control, these two approaches differ from standardized, government-mandated student assessments and from management- and expert-oriented models of assessment in their respect for students, teachers, and stakeholders as the proper locus of judgment and control regarding their own lives and endeavors.

This shared ethic far from guarantees the acceptance of either personalized assessment or responsive evaluation, both of which are minor players on their neighboring stages. The ethic, the empowerment, the epistemology, the validity, the flexibility are nonetheless important wherever personalization and responsiveness have opportunity to contribute. These approaches are critical as viable, provocative alternatives to better established but more exclusionary, authoritarian approaches.

Notes

1. My answer to each of the multiple-choice analogies in this text would be *c*. Do you disagree? Consider the arbitrariness of many so-called right answers and the implication of that arbitrariness for whether or not multiple-choice tests really are, as they are often termed, objective.

2. This discussion follows Samuel Messick's definition: "Validity is an integrated evaluative judgment of the degree to which empirical evidence and theoretical rationales support the *adequacy* and *appropriateness* of *inferences* and *actions* based on test scores or other modes of assessment. . . . Validity is an inductive summary of both the existing evidence for and the potential consequences of score interpretation and use. Hence, what is to be validated is not the test or observation device as such, but the inferences derived from test scores or other indicators—inferences about score meaning or interpretation and about the implications for action that the interpretation entails" (1989, p. 13, emphasis in the original).

References

American Educational Research Association, American Psychological Association, and National Council on Measurement in Education. *Standards for Educational and Psychological Testing.* Washington, D.C.: American Educational Research Association, 1999.

Berlak, H. "Toward the Development of a New Science of Educational Testing and Assessment." In H. Berlak and others (eds.), *Toward a New Science of Educational Testing and Assessment.* Albany: State University of New York Press, 1992.

Boser, U. "Standards-Related Policies: Pressure Without Support." In *Quality Counts 2001: A Better Balance* (a report on education in the 50 states by the 2001 Editorial Projects in Education). *Education Week*, 2001, *20*(17), 68–84.

Elmore, R., and others. "Holding Accountability Systems Accountable: Research-Based Standards." Presentation at the annual meeting of the American Educational Research Association, Seattle, Wash., Apr. 2001.

Erikson, E. H. *Childhood and Society.* (2nd ed.) New York: Norton, 1963.

Gardner, H. *Frames of Mind: The Theory of Multiple Intelligences.* New York: Basic Books, 1983.

Glaberson, W. "U.S. Court Says Awards Based on S.A.T.'s Are Unfair to Girls." *New York Times*, Feb. 4, 1989, pp. 1, 50.

Goertz, M. "The Long March: School Performance Goals and Progress Measures in State Accountability Systems." Paper presented at the annual meeting of the American Evaluation Research Association, Seattle, Wash., Apr. 2001.

Haladyna, T. M., Nolen, S. B., and Haas, N. S. "Raising Standardized Achievement Test Scores and the Origins of Test Score Pollution." *Educational Researcher*, 1991, *20*(5), 2–7.

Hillocks, G. "How State Mandatory Assessment Simplifies Writing Instruction in Illinois and Texas." Paper presented at the annual meeting of the American Educational Research Association, Chicago, Mar. 1997.

Impara, J. C., and Plake, B. S. "Standard Setting: Variation on a Theme by Anghoff." Paper presented at the annual meeting of the American Educational Research Association, Chicago, Mar. 1997.

Kane, M. "Validating the Performance Standards Associated with Passing Scores." *Review of Educational Research*, 1994, *64*(3), 425–561.

Kohlberg, L. *The Psychology of Moral Development.* San Francisco: HarperCollins, 1984.

Koretz, D. "Toward a Framework for Evaluating Gains on High-Stakes Tests." Paper presented at the annual meeting of the National Council on Measurement in Education, Seattle, Wash., Apr. 2001.

Mabry, L. "Performance Assessment and Inferences of Achievement." Unpublished doctoral dissertation, University of Illinois at Urbana-Champaign, 1995.

Mabry, L. (ed.) *Advances in Program Evaluation, Vol. 3: Evaluation and the Post-Modern Dilemma.* Greenwich, Conn.: JAI Press, 1997.

Mabry, L. *Portfolios Plus: A Critical Guide to Alternative Assessments and Portfolios.* Thousand Oaks, Calif.: Corwin Press, 1999a.

Mabry, L. "Writing to the Rubric: Lingering Effects of Traditional Testing on Direct Writing Assessment." *Phi Delta Kappan*, 1999b, *80*(9), 673–679.

Madaus, G. F., Scriven, M. S., and Stufflebeam, D. L. (eds.). *Evaluation Models: Viewpoints on Educational and Human Services Evaluation.* Boston: Kluwer-Nijhoff, 1987.

Messick, S. "Validity." In R. L. Linn (ed.), *Educational Measurement.* (3rd ed.) New York: American Council on Education, Macmillan, 1989.

Piaget, J. *The Language and Thought of the Child.* New York: World, 1955.

Popham, W. J. "Standard Setting: What Really Sways the Setters?" Paper presented at the annual meeting of the American Educational Research Association, San Francisco, Apr. 1995.

Scriven, M. *Evaluation Thesaurus.* (4th ed.) Thousand Oaks, Calif.: Sage, 1991.

Scriven, M. "An Evaluation Dilemma: Change Agent vs. Analyst." Paper presented at the annual meeting of the American Evaluation Association, Chicago, Nov. 1998.

Shadish, W. R., Jr., Cook, T. D., and Leviton, L. C. *Foundations of Program Evaluation: Theories of Practice.* Thousand Oaks, Calif.: Sage, 1991.

Smith, N. "Professional Reasons for Declining an Evaluation Contract." *American Journal of Evaluation*, 1998, *19*(2), 177–190.

Stake, R. E. *Evaluating the Arts in Education: A Responsive Approach.* Columbus, Ohio: Merrill, 1975.

Stake, R. E. "Program Evaluation, Particularly Responsive Evaluation." Keynote address at the conference "New Trends in Evaluation," Institute of Education, University of Göteborg, Sweden, Oct., 1973. In G. F. Madaus, M. S. Scriven, and D. L. Stufflebeam (eds.), *Evaluation Models: Viewpoints on Educational and Human Services Evaluation.* Boston: Kluwer-Nijhoff, 1987.

Stake, R. E. *The Invalidity of Standardized Testing for Measuring Mathematics Achievement.* Monograph for the National Center for Research on Mathematical Sciences Education. Madison: University of Wisconsin, 1991.

Stake, R. E., and others. "The Evolving Syntheses of Program Value," *Evaluation Practice,* 1997, *18*(2), 89–104.

Stake, R., and Pearsol, J. A. "Evaluating Responsively." In R. S. Brandt (ed.), *Applied Strategies for Curriculum Evaluation.* Alexandria, VA.: ASCD, 1981.

Stiggins, R. J., and Conklin, N. F. *In Teachers' Hands: Investigating the Practices of Classroom Assessment.* Albany: State University of New York Press, 1992.

Stufflebeam, D. L., Madaus, G. F., and Kellaghan, T. (eds.). *Evaluation Models: Viewpoints on Educational and Human Services Evaluation.* (2nd ed.) Boston: Kluwer, 2000.

Vygotsky, L. S. *Mind in Society: The Development of Higher Mental Process.* Cambridge, Mass.: Harvard University Press, 1978.

Worthen, B. R., Sanders, J. R., and Fitzpatrick, J. L. *Program Evaluation: Alternative Approaches and Practical Guidelines.* (2nd ed.) New York: Longman, 1997.

LINDA MABRY *is an assessment researcher and program evaluator at Washington State University Vancouver.*

INDEX

Back Issue/Subscription Order Form

Copy or detach and send to:
Jossey-Bass, 989 Market Street, San Francisco CA 94103-1741

Call or fax toll free!
Phone 888-378-2537 6AM-5PM PST; Fax 800-605-2665

Back issues: Please send me the following issues at $27 each.
(Important: please include series initials and issue number, such as EV77.)

1. EV _____

_____

_____

$ _____ Total for single issues

$ _____ Shipping charges (for single issues *only;* subscriptions are exempt
from shipping charges): Up to $30, add $5^{50} • $30^{01}–$50, add $6^{50}
$50^{01}–$75, add $7^{50} • $75^{01}–$100, add $9 • $100^{01}–$150, add $10
Over $150, call for shipping charge.

Subscriptions   Please ❑ start   ❑ renew my subscription to *New Directions
for Evaluation* for the year ___ at the following rate:

❑ Individual: $69 U.S./Canada/Mexico; $93 International

❑ Institutional: $145 U.S.; $185 Canada; $219 International
NOTE: Subscriptions are quarterly, and are for the calendar year only.
Subscriptions begin with the spring issue of the year indicated above.
For shipping outside the U.S., please add $25.
Prices are subject to change.

$ _____ Total single issues and subscriptions (CA, IN, NJ, NY and DC
residents, add sales tax for single issues. NY and DC residents must
include shipping charges when calculating sales tax. NY and Canadian
residents only, add sales tax for subscriptions.)

❑ Payment enclosed (U.S. check or money order only.)
❑ VISA, MC, AmEx, Discover Card # _____ Exp. date _____

Signature _____ Day phone _____
❑ Bill me (U.S. institutional orders only. Purchase order required.)
Purchase order # _____

Name _____

Address _____

_____

Phone _____ E-mail _____

For more information about Jossey-Bass, visit our Web site at:
www.josseybass.com   **PRIORITY CODE = ND1**

OTHER TITLES AVAILABLE IN THE
NEW DIRECTIONS FOR EVALUATION SERIES
Jennifer C. Greene, Gary T. Henry, Editors-in-Chief